Contents

STUFF TO WEAR

STUFF TO CREATE

STUFF FOR FUN

ART PR

STUFF FOR A PARTY

STUFF FOR YOUR ROOM

If you love everything *Star Wars* and can't get enough, this is the book for you! Inside you'll find ways to turn ordinary stuff into amazing intergalactic creations.

Whether you're a Jedi novice or a master of the Force, it doesn't make a difference—there are ideas that are guaranteed to inspire you and stretch your creativity.

We'll show you amazing ways to make all kinds of toys, puppets, wearable art, and even party favors featuring your favorite *Star Wars* characters and technology. You'll be able to decorate your room, put on a show, and even dress like Princess Leia or the fiercest Jedi warrior. Filled with awesome facts and fun tips, the ideas in this book will help you explore the *Star Wars* universe in a new way.

Ready to journey through a crafts galaxy? Well, let's get started...

AND MAY THE FORCE BE WITH YOU!

No skills? No sweat! This symbol marks our simplest projects.

Crafting Rock Star? This symbol marks our harder projects.

Careful! This symbol marks the materials that require adult supervision for safety.

STUFF TO WEAR

Gamorrean Guard Mask

They may not be the brightest porcine humanoids in the galaxy, but Gamorreans are fierce fighters. They're often hired as bounty hunters and guards because of their brute strength. You can make your own Gamorrean mask and scare off any intruders, too!

WHAT YOU NEED:

- ✓ 2 white paper plates
- ✓ Pencil
- ✓ Scissors
- ✓ White duct tape
- ✓ Olive green craft paint
- ✓ Paintbrush
- ✓ Brown, white, and black construction paper
- ✓ Ruler
- ✓ Black marker
- ✓ Glue stick
- ✓ Craft knife
- ✓ 4 rubber bands

1 Place both plates upside down. Place one plate over the second plate, covering the bottom one about halfway. Use a pencil to trace around the rim of the top plate.

2 Cut along the pencil line, and set the bottom piece aside.

3 Tape the whole plate and the top of the second plate together, with the tape at the back.

4 Paint the plates Gamorrean green and set aside to dry.

5 Draw a figure eight onto the brown paper measuring approximately 18 cm x 5 cm. Below that, draw a 10 cm diamond. Draw two nostrils with black marker on the diamond.

USE THE FORCE!

To make the figure eight the right size, you can measure out a rectangle first, marking the dimensions with a pencil for guidance.

6 On white paper, draw two horns for the top of the head, two large teeth about 5 cm tall, and two smaller teeth.

7 Cut out the figure eight, leaving a 1 cm border around the entire shape. Color in the figure eight with black marker and use a glue stick to attach the teeth to make a scary mouth.

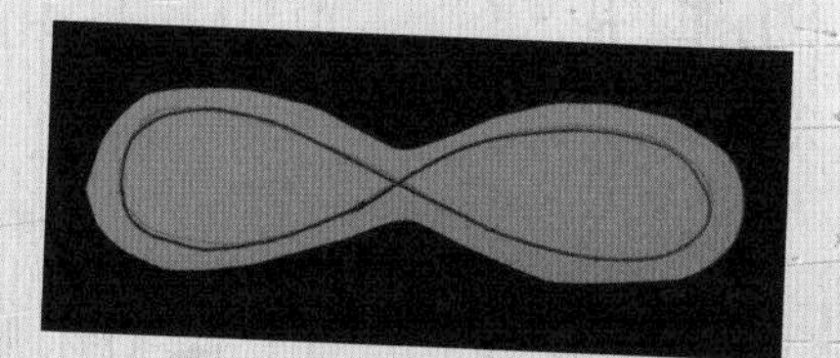

8 From black paper, cut a triangle for the top of the helmet almost as tall as the top plate, and cut out two curved side pieces to fit.

9 Assemble the mask by gluing on the mouth and nose first. Next, attach the top of the helmet, then the horns and sides of the helmet.

10 Make a template for the eyeholes. Take the remaining piece of paper plate you set aside in step 2, and hold it up to your face. Have a friend use a pencil to mark the plate where your eyes are. Use a craft knife to cut two almond shapes and hold it up to your face to check if the spacing is right. When it is, use this as a template to cut eyeholes in your mask.

11 To keep the mask on your head, create a rubber band chain with four rubber bands by looping them through each other. Staple an end to each side of the mask above your ears, and cover the staples with duct tape.

WHAT YOU NEED:

- ✓ 6–10 small boxes (empty juice boxes work great)
- ✓ Scrap paper
- ✓ Silver and brown duct tape
- ✓ Craft knife
- ✓ Cutting mat

Chewbacca's Bandolier

Chewbacca, Han Solo's Wookiee co-pilot, is always ready for action, carrying extra supplies in a bandolier strapped across his body. This one has a handy bag at the end, just at arm's length!

1 Stuff boxes with crumpled scrap paper so that they don't collapse. Cover boxes with silver duct tape. (You can vary the sizes by cutting some of the boxes down.)

2 Working on a cutting mat, measure and cut four 38 cm-long strips of brown tape. Stick one strip on your mat. Stick a second strip down, overlapping the long edges by about ½ cm to layer the strips together. Repeat with the other strips. Lift the sheet off the mat and turn it over, sticky side up. Bring the bottom, long edge up and stick it down around the center mark, as shown. Bring the top section down and stick it slightly overlapping the first to create the bandolier belt. You will need a total of four of these folded sheets (three for younger kids).

3 Connect these four sheets together, end to end, using additional pieces of brown tape.

4 Roll small pieces of tape, sticky side out, and use them to attach the ammo boxes to the brown belt, leaving about 2½ to 5 cm between each box.

5 Measure and cut four 38 cm-long strips of brown tape. With one strip sticky side up, fold a third of the tape lengthwise up onto itself. Fold the other third down onto that to create a thin strip. Repeat for the other three strips. Connect all four strips together using additional brown tape.

6 Attach the thin strip across the top of the ammo boxes, tucking it down snugly between each box using additional brown tape. Save any excess to use as the handle for the bag.

7 To make the bag, repeat step 2 to make a sheet, this time using six strips of tape. With the sheet sticky side up, fold it almost in half, leaving about 1 cm or so of exposed sticky tape. Fold that sticky edge down to complete the sheet.

8 Measure and cut a 40 cm strip of brown tape. Cut that strip in half lengthwise. Cut one of those in half again. Use those two pieces to close the edges of the bag by folding the sheet in half and taping the sides together.

9 For the bag flap, cut a 5 cm-long section from one side of the opening of the bag. Fold the other side down and tape the bag closed.

10 Use the leftover strip from step 6 to create the bag handle. Open the bag and tape the strip inside under the flap.

11 Place the bandolier over your shoulder to get a feel for the fit. Trim if needed. Tape the bag straps to the ends of the bandolier belt.

WHAT YOU NEED:

- ✓ White and silver duct tape
- ✓ Craft knife
- ✓ Cutting mat
- ✓ 5 small coins

Princess Leia's Belt

As an Imperial Senator, Princess Leia wears a white dress with a belt around her waist. You can make your own belt, just like Princess Leia's, with some duct tape and 5 small coins!

1 Make a 45 cm-long duct tape sheet using five strips of white duct tape (see step 2 on page 8).

2 Turn the sheet upside down, so the sticky side is facing up, and fold it in thirds onto itself.

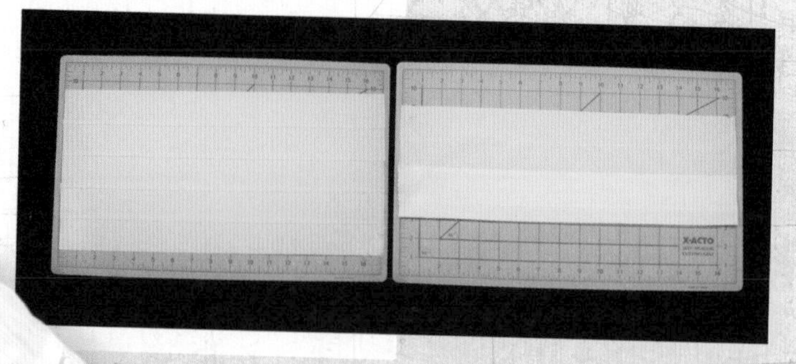

3 Repeat steps 1 and 2 until you have the length you need to wrap around your waist. Connect the pieces using additional tape.

4 Make a 15 cm-long duct tape sheet using three strips of white duct tape.

5 Turn the sheet upside down and fold it into thirds onto itself.

6 Use a craft knife to cut the left and right side off at a diagonal, making a triangle.

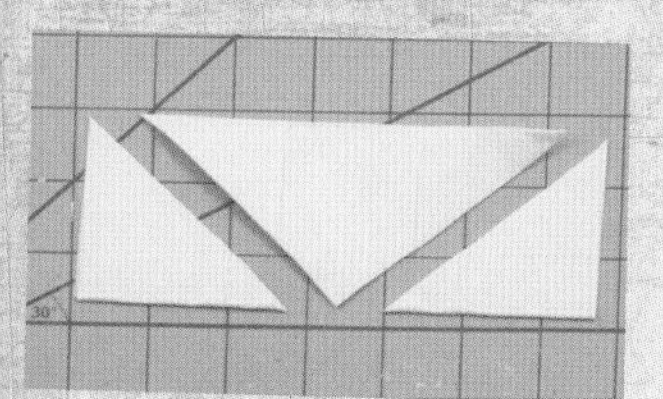

7 Tape the triangle to the front of the belt in the center.

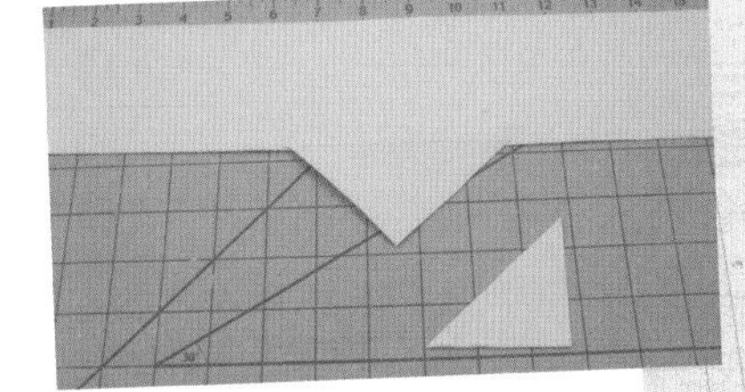

8 Make a 10 cm-long duct tape sheet, using two strips of silver duct tape.

9 Use a craft knife to cut out a pentagon, point side down, as shown. Stick this to the triangle on the belt.

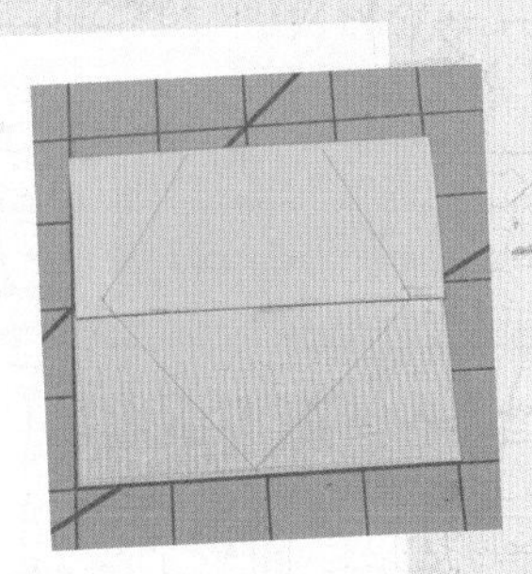

10 Make another 10 cm-long duct tape sheet in silver.

11 Use a craft knife to cut out an octagon that is wider than it is tall.

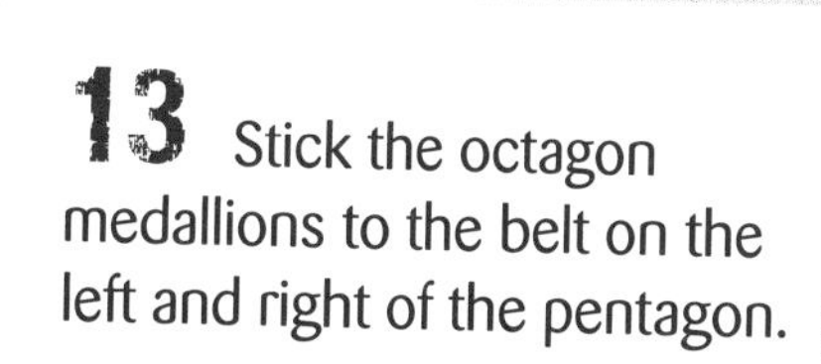

12 Repeat steps 10 and 11 three more times, making four octagon medallions.

13 Stick the octagon medallions to the belt on the left and right of the pentagon.

14 Measure and cut a 30 cm piece of silver duct tape and turn it sticky side up. Place the coins onto the sticky side of the tape, evenly spaced apart from each other. Use a craft knife to cut the strip of tape into sections, one coin per section.

15 Wrap the tape around each coin, covering them completely. Roll a small piece of duct tape, sticky side out, and use it to attach each covered coin to the center of each medallion.

FUN FACT:

Dedicated to the Rebel Alliance and an excellent shot with a blaster, Princess Leia of Alderaan is tough and beautiful, fighting alongside Luke Skywalker and Han Solo.

WHAT YOU NEED:

- ✓ Duct tape: black, brown, silver
- ✓ Cutting mat
- ✓ Craft knife
- ✓ 10 cm cardboard tube

Han Solo's Vest & Belt

You, too, can be the smuggler turned hero, Han Solo, who helped destroy the Death Star alongside Luke Skywalker. Dress up as Han by making your own vest and belt!

For the vest:

1 You'll need to make three or four double-sided duct tape sheets out of black duct tape. Here's how: Roll out a piece of tape 43 cm long. Stick it down lightly to your work surface. Stick a second strip down, overlapping the first strip about ½ cm. Repeat until you have a sheet made up of six strips. Set this sheet aside, and make a second sheet the same size.

2 Line these sheets up, matching the long sides, and tape them together to make a really big sheet.

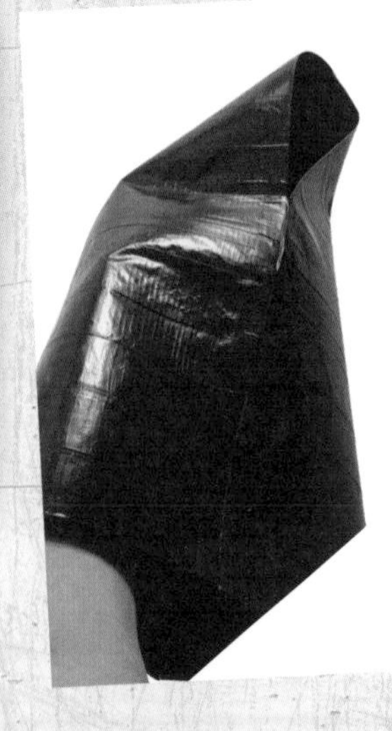

3 Fold the long sheet in half so the short ends match. Starting from the bottom corner, tape these sheets together, stopping when you get two-thirds of the way up, so you leave an open section as an armhole. Repeat on the other side.

4 Put the vest on your work surface as shown, with the armholes on the side. Use scissors to cut straight up the middle of the front panel, as shown. Stop cutting when you reach the fold at the top.

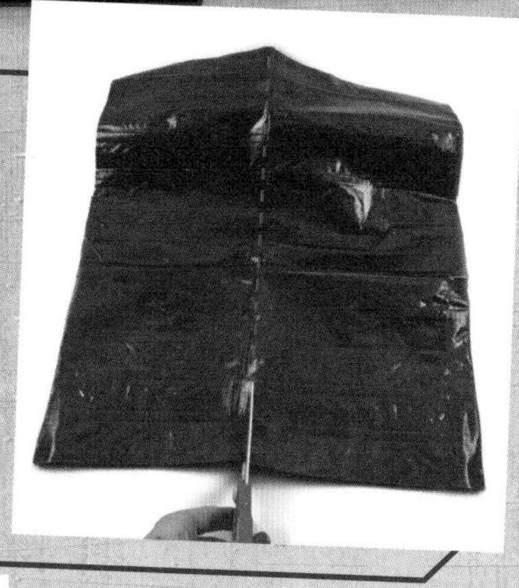

5 From each side of the opening, cut off a strip around 2 cm wide, all the way up the front of the vest, stopping when you get to the fold at the top. Cut these strips off and set them aside.

6 Cut a curve at the top of the vest for the neck area.

7 Use the strips you saved from step 5 to make pocket flaps. Cut them into four 13 cm pieces.

8 Roll a piece of duct tape, sticky side out, and attach it to a pocket flap piece, as shown. Turn it over and press it onto the front of the vest. Place two pocket flaps on each side.

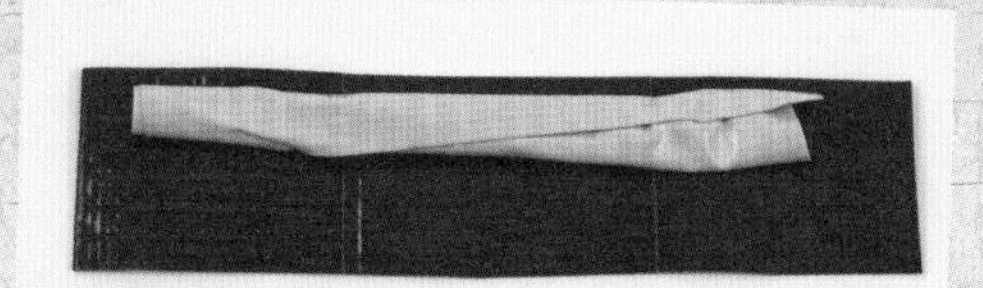

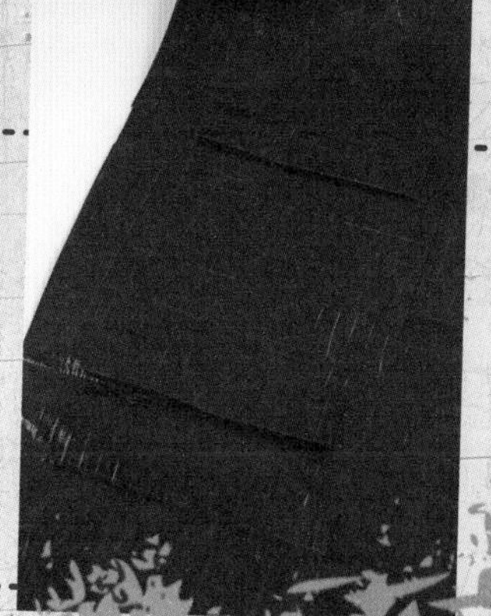

FUN FACT:

Han Solo was a smuggler and a troublemaker who, with his Wookiee sidekick, Chewbacca, is on the run from a bounty hunter when he first meets Luke Skywalker and Obi-Wan Kenobi. But once he learns about the plight of the Rebel Alliance, he becomes one of its most dedicated supporters, fighting for the cause of galactic freedom.

USE THE FORCE!

You can trim the armholes to make them deeper if that will be more comfortable. If your vest is too tight or too loose, you can cut up the center of the back of the vest to add or remove tape!

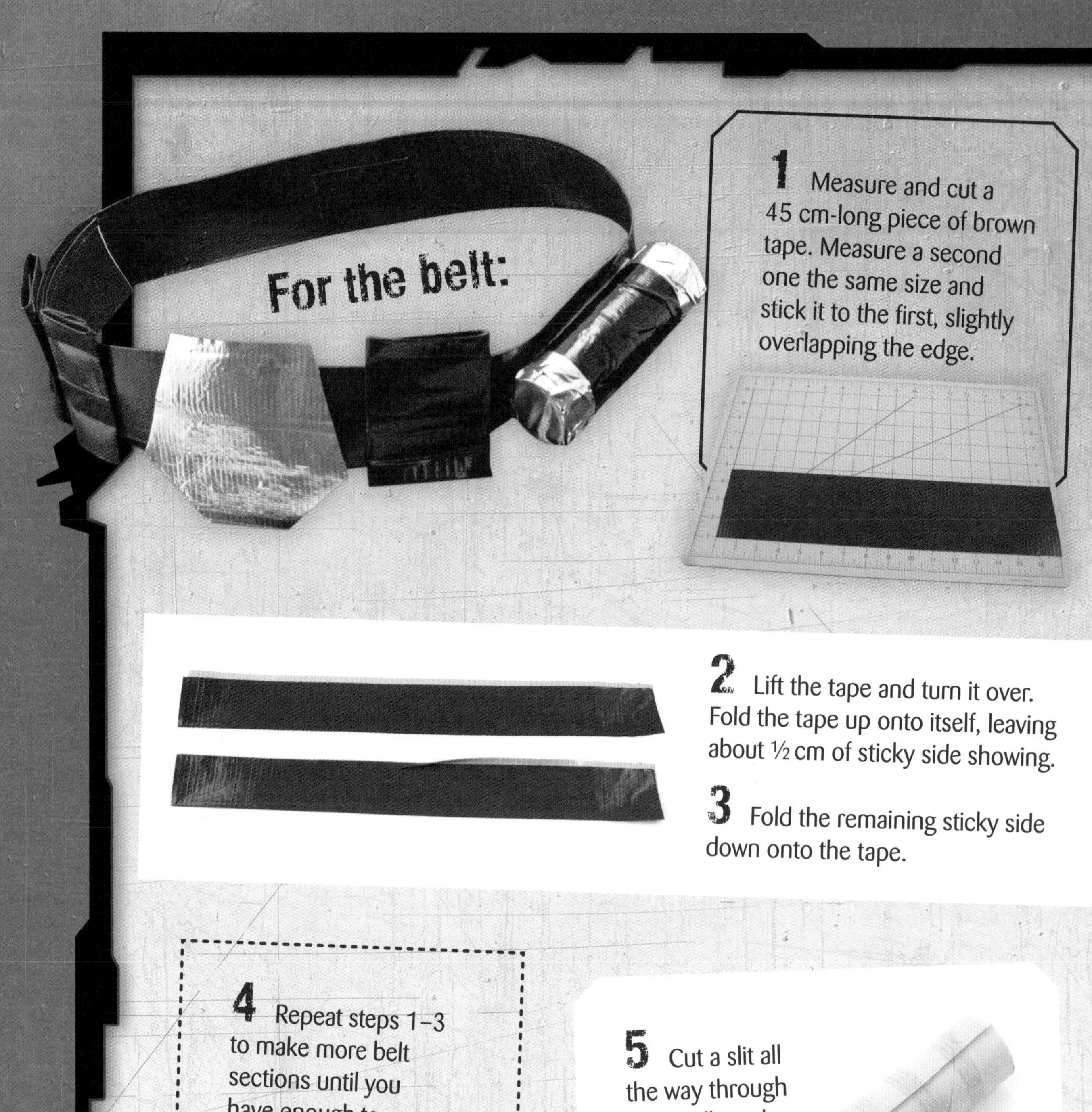

For the belt:

1 Measure and cut a 45 cm-long piece of brown tape. Measure a second one the same size and stick it to the first, slightly overlapping the edge.

2 Lift the tape and turn it over. Fold the tape up onto itself, leaving about ½ cm of sticky side showing.

3 Fold the remaining sticky side down onto the tape.

4 Repeat steps 1–3 to make more belt sections until you have enough to wrap around your waist. Join them together with additional brown tape.

5 Cut a slit all the way through the cardboard tube lengthwise to open it up.

6 Roll the tube up tighter than its original size and tape it to secure.

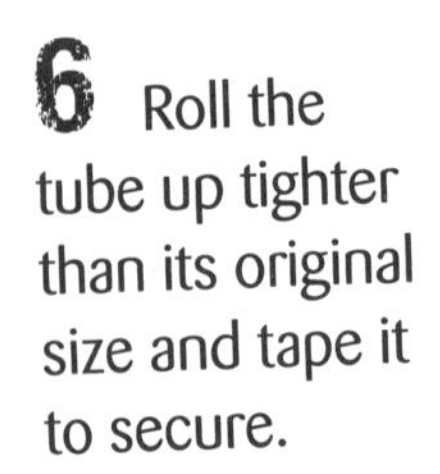

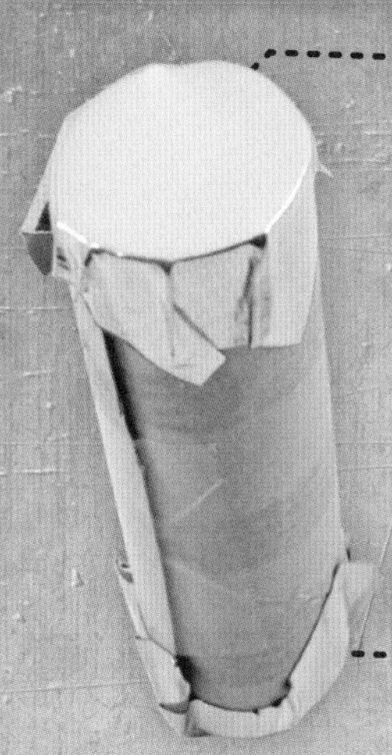

7 Cover the ends of the tube with silver duct tape. Then cover the rest of the tube with silver tape.

8 Wrap the center of the tube with black duct tape. Roll a piece of tape, sticky side out, and use it to attach the weapon holster to the belt.

9 For the belt buckle, create a 20 cm long silver tape sheet, three strips high.

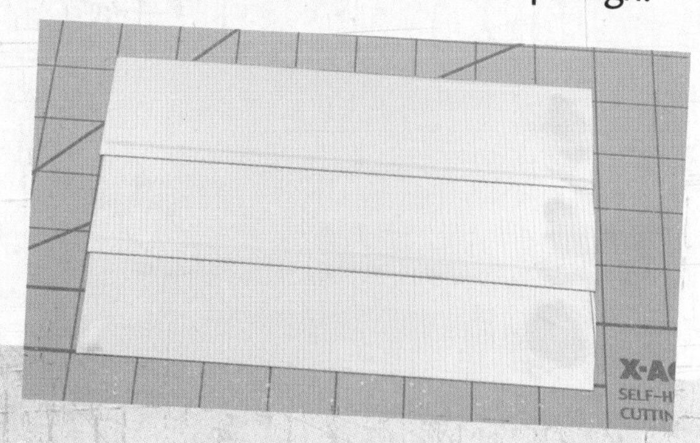

10 Lift the tape from the cutting mat, turn it over, and fold it in half as shown.

11 Use a craft knife to cut the silver sheet into an irregular hexagon. Use rolled tape to attach it to the front of the belt.

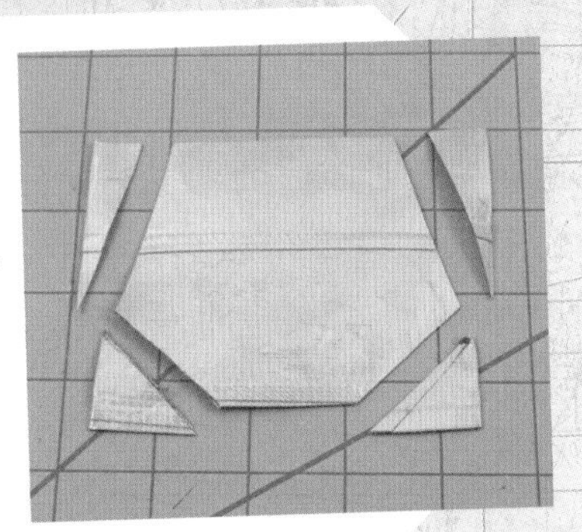

12 Using brown duct tape, attach two 13 cm strips together, sticky side to sticky side. Fold in thirds and tape together. Attach to the belt with rolled tape. This is your ammo pouch.

13 Repeat step 12 two more times to complete the belt.

FUN FACT:

When Princess Leia first meets her rescuers, Han Solo and Luke Skywalker, she isn't very impressed by them. But as time goes on, she comes to recognize their many good qualities.

Galaxy Hat

Turn an ordinary black hat into a cap that's out of this world! Making your own galaxy is a lot easier than you might think.

WHAT YOU NEED:

- ✓ Acrylic craft paint: light purple, light blue, dark blue, white
- ✓ Old toothbrush
- ✓ 1 sheet construction paper in a dark color
- ✓ Large paintbrush
- ✓ Paper towel or old rag
- ✓ Black baseball cap
- ✓ Toothpick

1 Combine two teaspoons of white paint and ¼ teaspoon of water in a dish. Stir to combine with the toothbrush.

2 Practice your technique on some construction paper first. Place the construction paper on a table and dip the bristles of the toothbrush into the thinned white paint. Press the toothbrush (still full of paint) into the paper towel to remove excess paint. Then, with the bristles over the construction paper and pointing down, drag your thumb or finger across the bristles, releasing speckles of paint to the paper. Practice this a few times before moving to the cap.

3 When you're ready, use the method in step 2 to apply the background stars to your black cap.

4 Dip the paintbrush into purple paint. Press the paintbrush into the paper towel and move it in a circular motion to remove most of the paint. Rub the "dry" brush on the cap in different areas to create splotches.

5 Repeat step 4 with light blue paint and again with blue paint.

6 Repeat step 3 with white paint for more stars over the blue paint.

7 Dip a toothpick into white paint and dot paint onto the cap to add some bright stars in random areas.

Princess Leia's Bracelet & Necklace

Princess Leia Organa wears the ceremonial necklace during the Royal Award Ceremony to honor the heroes of Yavin. It is polished to a bright silver finish, and has fourteen square pieces. You can make your own, adding or removing squares to make it fit you.

WHAT YOU NEED:

- ✓ Empty cardboard roll from duct tape
- ✓ Scissors
- ✓ Silver duct tape
- ✓ Cutting mat
- ✓ Craft knife
- ✓ 60 cm piece of yarn

USE THE FORCE!

You can use aluminium foil instead of duct tape for this project. Foil will bend more easily but duct tape will last longer.

1 Use scissors to cut the empty cardboard roll into a cuff that fits your wrist. Bend it into shape so that it fits well. Cover the cuff with silver duct tape.

2 On your cutting mat, measure and cut 7 cm-long pieces of silver duct tape. One 7 cm piece of tape will make one square of the necklace.

3 Turn the piece of tape over and fold it into thirds, sticking the tape to itself so that no sticky side remains.

4 Tape the yarn down to your cutting mat to secure it while you're working. Fold your tape pieces over the yarn and stick them together with thin, 1 cm strips of silver tape. This way the squares will move and hang freely on the necklace but they won't fall off.

5 Place the necklace around your neck, knot it, and trim off most of the excess yarn.

WHAT YOU NEED:

- ✓ White T-shirt
- ✓ Cardboard or a cardboard shirt form
- ✓ Fabric paints: red, blue, black, silver
- ✓ Silver 3-D fabric paint
- ✓ Paintbrush
- ✓ Pencil

R2-D2 T-Shirt

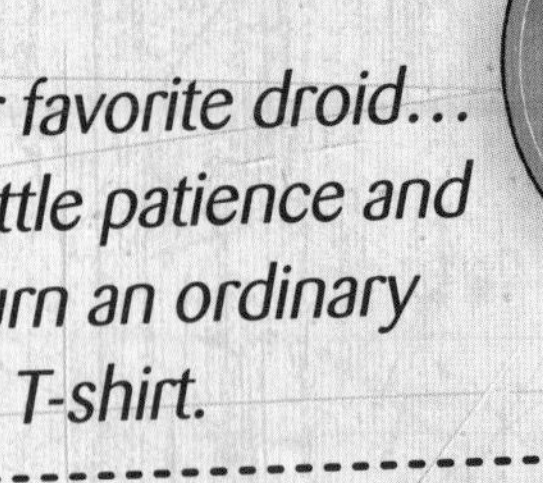

Now you can be your favorite droid… well, almost! With a little patience and some fabric paints, turn an ordinary T-shirt into an R2-D2 T-shirt.

1 Insert the cardboard inside the T-shirt to give you a flat surface to work on.

2 Use a pencil to lightly draw the shapes for your R2-D2 design.

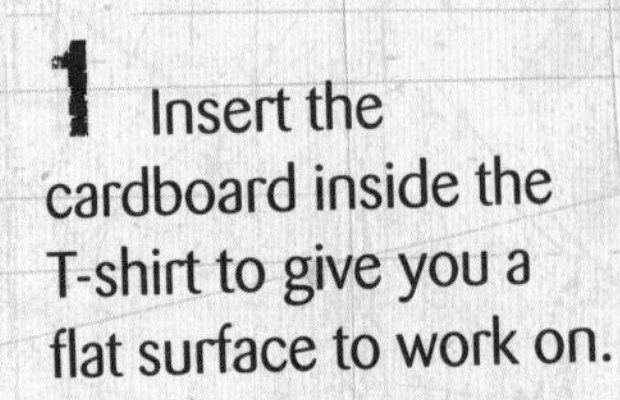

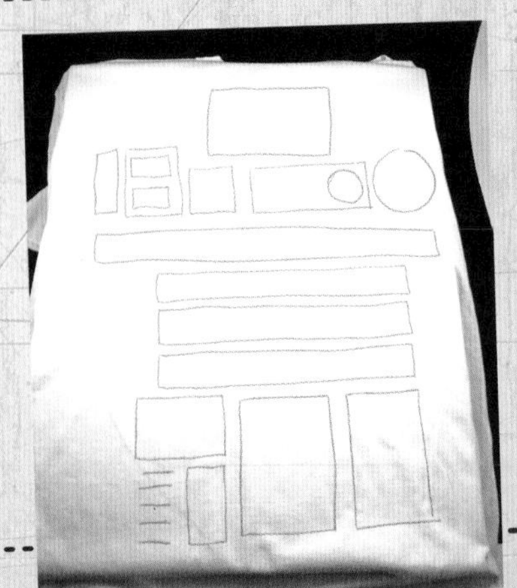

3 Paint each section with fabric paint.

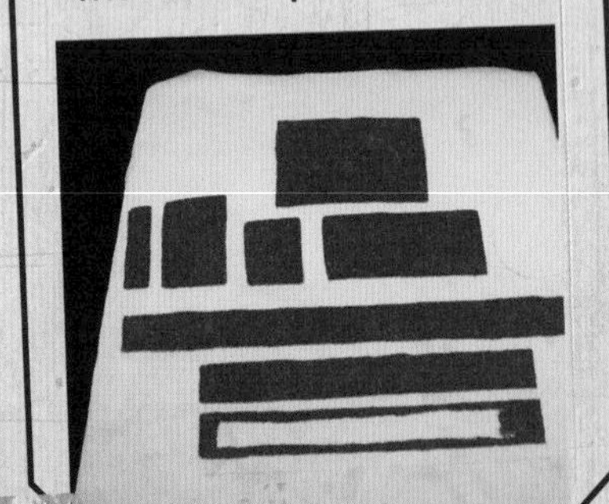

4 Use the 3-D paint to outline the holographic projector and the rectangles on the logic display and to draw the input receptors.

USE THE FORCE!

You can use a foam spouncer to create round accents.

5 Allow everything to dry overnight.

STUFF TO CREATE

WHAT YOU NEED:

- ✓ Empty cardboard snack box
- ✓ White faux fur
- ✓ Hot glue gun
- ✓ Felt: dark brown, red, black, white
- ✓ 2 large googly eyes
- ✓ Scissors

Snack Box Wampa

You can make your own tame wampa, who will be nothing like the fierce ice creatures from the planet Hoth. You can use any recycled box, making your wampa the size you want—in fact, you can make a family of wampas!

1 Cover the snack box, except for the bottom, in white faux fur, using your hot glue gun to attach the fur.

2 Cut C-shaped horns from dark brown felt, about the length of the box, and glue them to the top of the head and sides of the face.

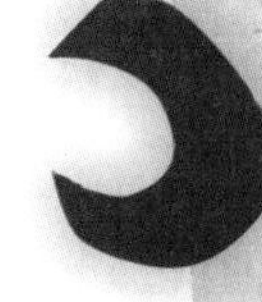

3 Cut an oval from black felt then cut another oval from red felt, about ½ cm smaller than the black one. Glue the red oval to the black oval.

4 Cut triangles from white felt for the teeth and glue them to the red oval. Glue the completed mouth to the front of the box.

5 Glue two large googly eyes above the mouth.

WHAT YOU NEED:

- ✓ Baking paper
- ✓ Baking tray
- ✓ ½ cup salt
- ✓ 1 cup flour
- ✓ ½ cup water
- ✓ Extra flour, if needed
- ✓ Paint: olive green, yellowish-tan, red-orange, black
- ✓ Black marker, gray marker

Salt Dough Jabba the Hutt

Jabba the Hutt lives in a palace on the planet Tatooine, from which he runs his criminal empire, employing smugglers like Han Solo. His sluglike alien shape and appearance are perfect for molding from salt dough!

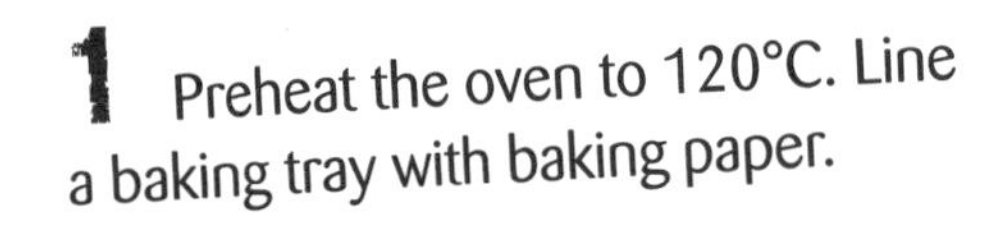

1 Preheat the oven to 120°C. Line a baking tray with baking paper.

2 In a bowl, stir together salt, flour, and water. If the dough is still sticky, add one teaspoon of additional flour at a time until the dough forms a ball when stirred.

3 Roll half the dough in your hands and shape it into a wide log on the parchment, tapering the end into a tail.

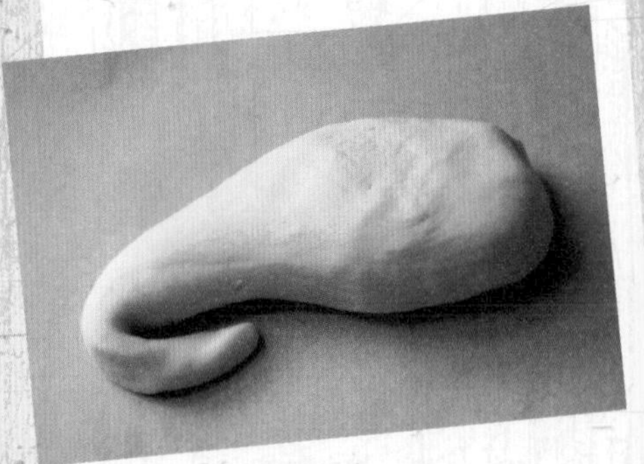

4 Roll three tablespoons of dough separately to create three balls. Flatten each one and layer them on top of each other to create Jabba's rolls.

5 Take ½ tablespoon of dough and break it into two pieces. Roll these to create the arms. Stick them to the sides. Roll the remaining dough into a ball, then shape the top into a soft point. Place it on top of the rolls.

6 Bake in the preheated oven for 2½ hours then allow to cool completely.

7 Paint the entire sculpture with yellowish-tan paint.

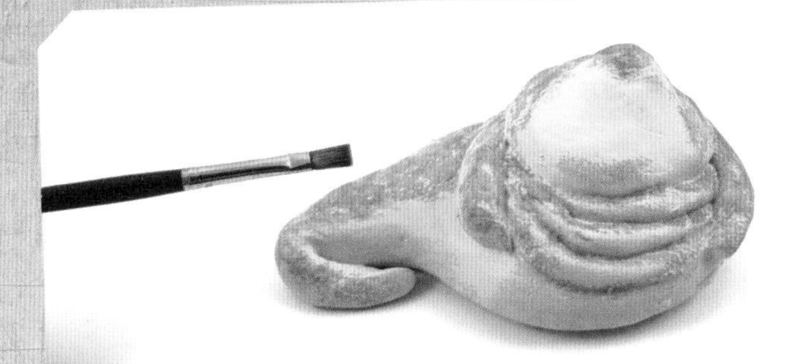

8 Dip a small paintbrush in olive green and dab the excess paint off onto a paper towel. Dry-brush the green paint along the top of the tail, the arms, the back and side of the head, and along the edges of the rolls.

9 Use a thin paintbrush with red-orange paint to add the eyes. Dot black paint in the center with the handle end of the paintbrush.

10 When the eyes are dry, trace around them with black marker. Add the eyebrows, nose, and mouth.

11 Use a gray marker to add lines along the tail and under the eyes and chin and to add some shading to the rolls and along the arms.

Tin Can C-3PO

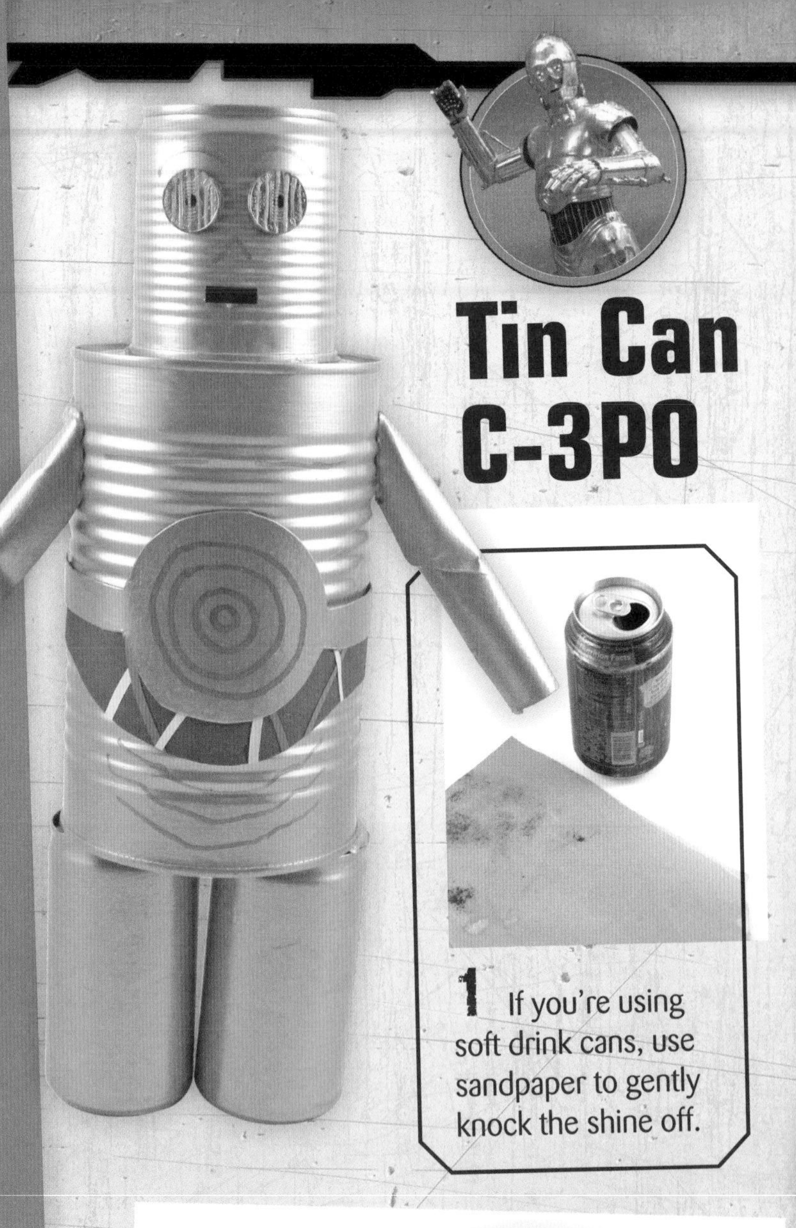

WHAT YOU NEED:

- ✓ 1 large vegetable can
- ✓ 2 small soft drink cans or tomato paste cans
- ✓ 1 small vegetable or fruit can
- ✓ Sandpaper
- ✓ 10 cm cardboard tube
- ✓ 15 cm square of cardboard (from a cereal box)
- ✓ Gold paint
- ✓ Hot glue gun
- ✓ Gold paint pen
- ✓ Construction paper: black, red, white, yellow
- ✓ Scissors
- ✓ Black marker
- ✓ White craft glue
- ✓ 5 small coins

C-3PO is a protocol droid, programmed to have great manners and to be fluent in many languages. Dedicated to his master, Luke Skywalker, and loyal friend to his partner droid, R2-D2, C-3PO was involved in many of their exploits, despite his cautious nature. Now you can have a droid by your side, too, once you build your own model C-3PO!

1 If you're using soft drink cans, use sandpaper to gently knock the shine off.

2 Paint the cardboard tube and cardboard square gold.

3 Paint the cans with a thin coat of gold paint. Let the cans dry for 30 min, then repeat for a second thin coat.

4 Give the cans a third coat and a fourth coat of gold paint if needed, allowing them to dry completely between coats.

5 From one edge of the gold cardboard, cut a rectangle to fit over the two small cans (which will be the legs) and hot glue it in place. Glue the large can to the cardboard, on top of the small cans, for the body.

6 Cut the round chest plate and belt from the gold cardboard.

7 Use a gold paint pen to draw circles onto the chest plate.

8 Cut a piece of black construction paper the length of the chest plate and belt with a curved bump to fit below the circle. Cut thin strips of red, yellow, and white paper to look like wires. Using white craft glue, attach them vertically onto the black paper.

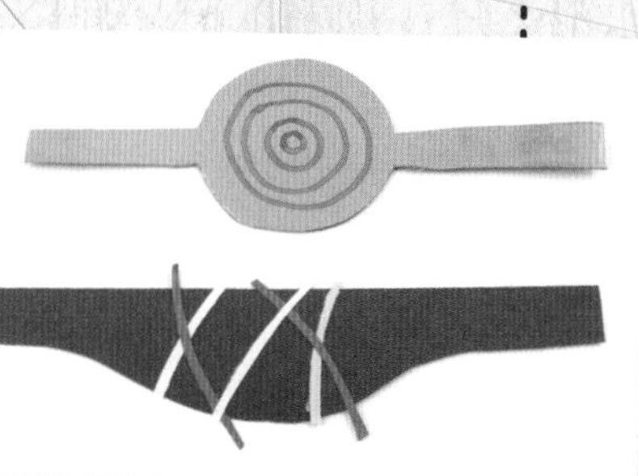

9 Glue the gold chest plate and belt onto the black paper, then hot glue the whole piece to the large can.

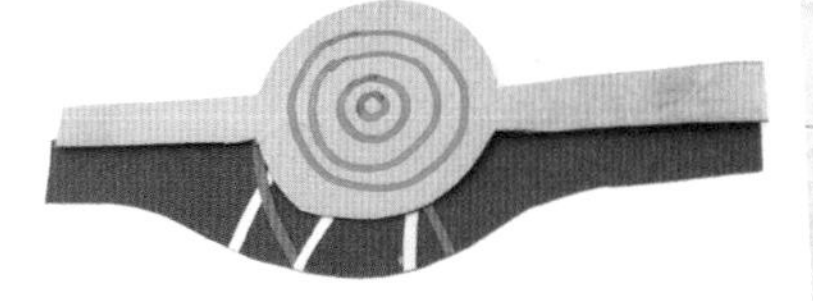

10 Cut the cardboard tube in half lengthwise. Roll each half into a narrow tube and glue together.

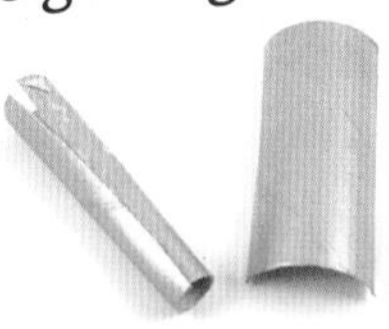

11 Cut a v-shaped notch at one end of each tube.

12 Glue the end with the v-shaped notch to the side of the can for the arms.

13 Place coins "tail" side up. Use a black marker to draw a dot in the center of each coin. Use a thin paintbrush to paint gold lines onto the coins.

14 Glue the coins to the small can for eyes.

15 Color a small piece of cardboard with black marker and cut out a small rectangle for the mouth, then glue it in place. Use a gold paint pen to add a nose and eyebrows.

WHAT YOU NEED:

- ✓ Brown construction paper (one sheet makes 2 Jawas)
- ✓ Pencil
- ✓ Scissors
- ✓ Tape
- ✓ Scraps of yellow and black construction paper
- ✓ Glue stick
- ✓ Gray or black marker

Paper Cone Jawas

These Jawas are super easy to make! You can create a whole clan and use them as placeholders for your next Star Wars *party. This is also a great project for the younger set.*

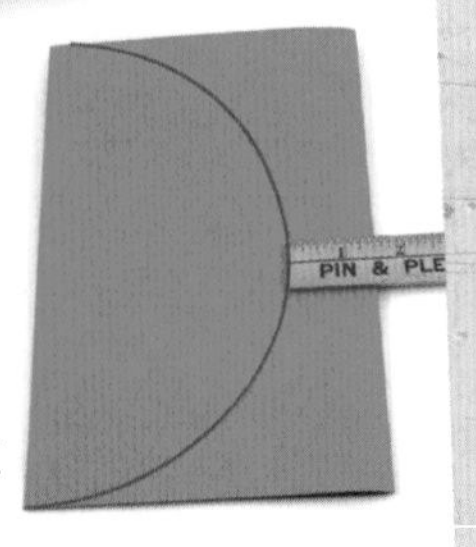

1 Fold the brown construction paper in half, like a book. Use a pencil to draw a half circle, starting from the free edge—the top of the circle should be about 4 cm from the fold.

2 Cut the two half circles from the paper and roll into cones, securing with tape.

3 Cut small ovals from black paper for faces and small rectangles from the yellow paper for the eyes.

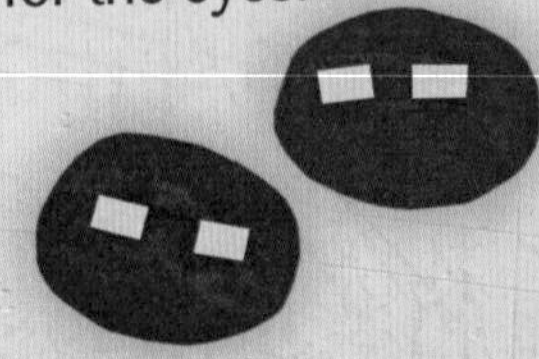

4 Glue the eyes to the black paper and glue the black paper to the front of the brown cones.

5 Using leftover brown paper, cut strips measuring 7½ cm x 1 cm to make the bandoliers.

6 Draw a border around the strips with marker and draw lines to make boxes for the ammo pouches. Draw the pouch flaps and add a dot for the pouch snaps.

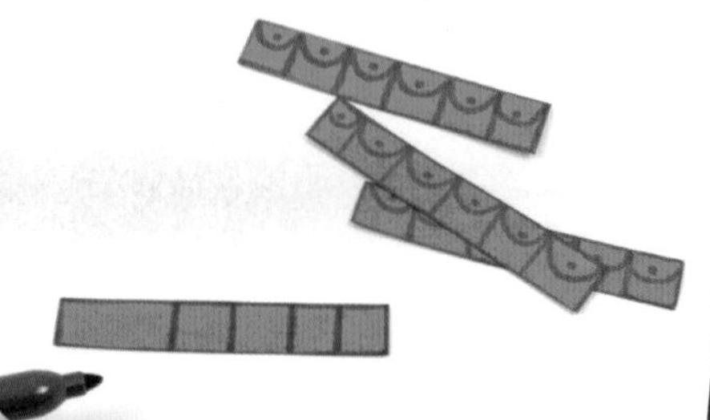

7 Glue the bandolier to the front of the cone.

WHAT YOU NEED:

- ✓ 10 cm cardboard tube
- ✓ Brown felt
- ✓ Tan, gray, or blue felt
- ✓ Scissors
- ✓ Felt glue (or a hot glue gun)
- ✓ 2 googly eyes
- ✓ Black marker
- ✓ Brown pipe cleaner
- ✓ Brown pom-pom

Cardboard Tube Ewoks

Ewoks may look like teddy bears, but they are fierce warriors who helped defeat the Empire in the Battle of Endor. Here's how to create a tribe of Ewoks for you and your friends.

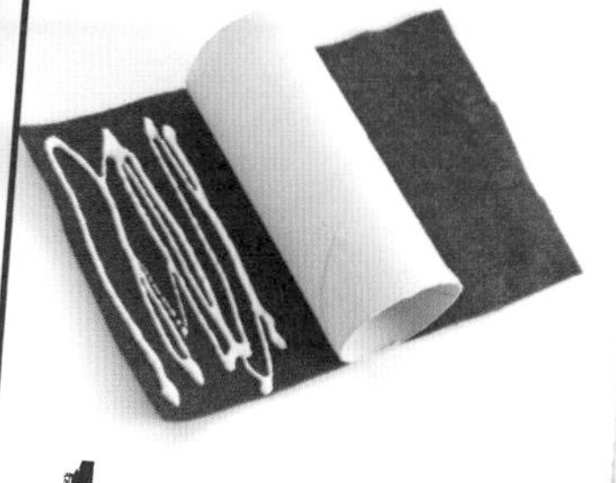

1 Cut some brown felt so it will wrap neatly around a cardboard tube. Glue it to the tube using felt glue or a hot glue gun.

2 Cut a 20 cm x 7½ cm rectangle out of tan, gray, or blue felt. Cut out an oval about 5 cm from the end.

3 Glue the rectangle over the top of the cardboard tube so that the oval is in front, where the face will be.

4 Cut two little circles from the brown felt for the ears. Trim one end straight across to make an ear shape. Glue the ears to the top of the Ewok's head.

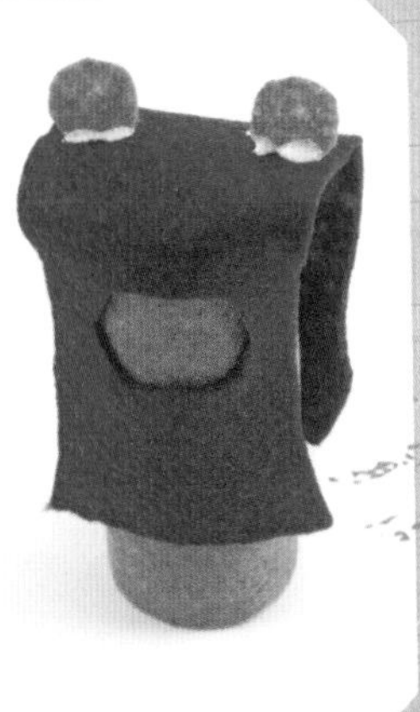

5 Glue googly eyes inside the oval shape. Use a fine-point marker to add "stitches" or a buckle on your Ewok's hood.

6 To give your Ewok a walking stick, cut a pipe cleaner in half, and glue it to a brown pom-pom. Glue the brown pom-pom onto your Ewok's side.

USE THE FORCE!

Felt glue is great when you're working with felt or other fabrics—and even pom-poms—because it doesn't soak through the fabric. It's easily available in craft stores and is nontoxic and washable.

WHAT YOU NEED:

- ✓ 30 cm dowel
- ✓ Craft knife
- ✓ 5½ cm Styrofoam ball
- ✓ Craft glue
- ✓ Craft paint: black, gray, white
- ✓ Cardboard snack or cracker box
- ✓ Scissors or cutting board
- ✓ Ruler
- ✓ Black and gray felt
- ✓ Silver or gray 3-D paint
- ✓ Hot glue gun
- ✓ 4 metal washers
- ✓ White colored pencil
- ✓ Pushpin
- ✓ String

Cardboard TIE Fighter

Make your own TIE fighter (or two or three!) and suspend your flying battalion from your bedroom ceiling. All you need are a few simple supplies!

1 Cut 7 cm off of the dowel so that it measures 23 cm. Insert the dowel through the center of the Styrofoam ball. Add some craft glue at the ends to secure it in place.

2 Mix 1 part gray paint with 5 parts white to get a muted gray color. Paint the Styrofoam ball and the dowel with this mixture and set aside to dry.

3 Cut the box apart—you'll need the front and back panels. Each panel should measure 23 cm x 15 cm.

4 Use a ruler to draw a straight line horizontally through the center of the panel.

5 Make pencil markings 2½ cm from each corner.

6 Draw a line from the upper left mark to the lower right mark. Repeat for the upper right and lower left marks.

7 Draw a line from the upper left mark down to the center line at the side. Repeat this for each corner, drawing a line to the center. Trim off the four corner diagonal pieces.

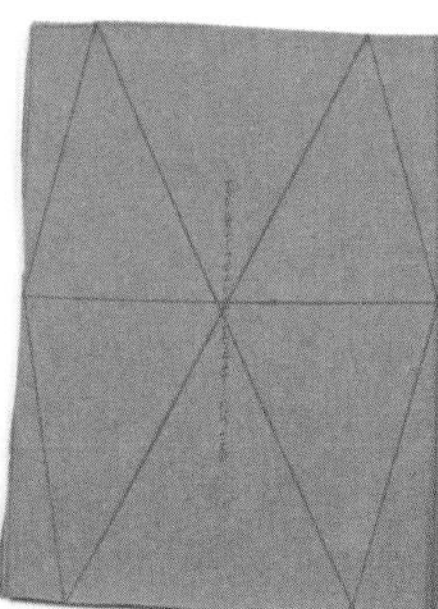

8 Repeat steps 4 through 7 for the second panel.

9 Use a craft knife to carefully lift the shiny paper from the front of the box panels.

USE THE FORCE!

It can be tricky to peel the box apart. Here's an option—you can simply sand the shine off with some sand paper.

10 Paint one side of both panels black and set aside to dry. Repeat for the other side.

11 Cut a circle from black felt measuring 4 cm in diameter.

12 Use 3-D paint to draw a circle in the center. Add eight equally spaced lines (like sunrays) coming from the center circle to the edge of the felt circle. Allow the 3-D paint to dry completely.

13 When dry, use craft glue to attach the black felt circle to the gray Styrofoam ball to create the cockpit.

14 Use a white colored pencil to draw lines onto the black panels, just like you did in steps 4, 6, and 7. Outline the panels with pencil as well.

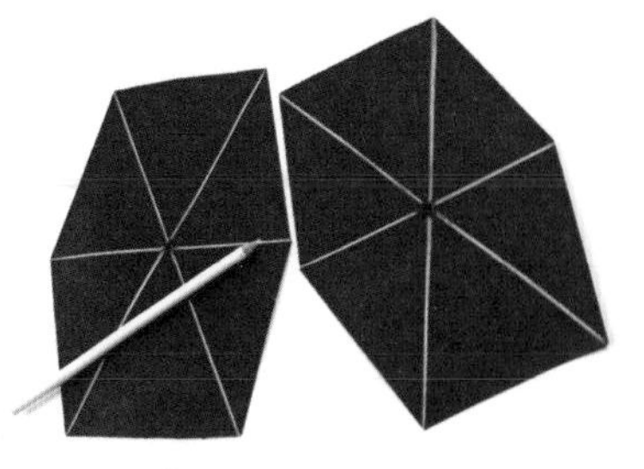

15 Use hot glue to stick a washer to each side of the panel at the center. Poke a hole through the center of the washer. Repeat for second panel.

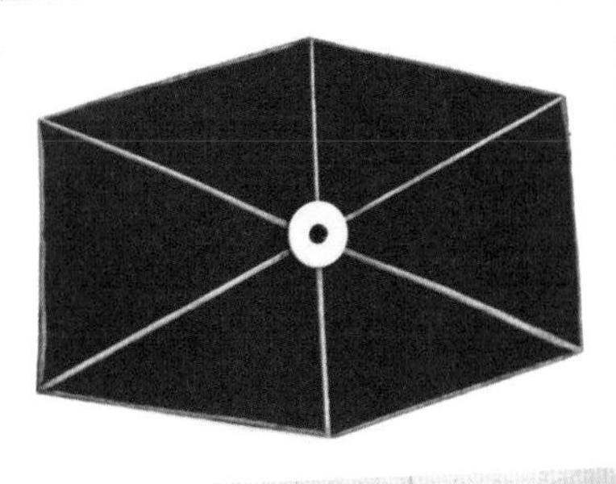

16 Add some hot glue to the center of the washer and insert one end of the dowel. Be sure that the cockpit window is lined up correctly. Repeat for the other panel. Secure with additional glue if needed.

17 If you want to hang your TIE fighter up, this is how you do it. Tie a piece of string to a pushpin and secure with hot glue. Add some hot glue to the top of the cockpit and push the pushpin into the glue.

FUN FACT:

TIE fighters are named for their engine technology—TIE stands for "twin ion engine." They're super-fast and super-maneuverable, but they offer little protection for their pilots.

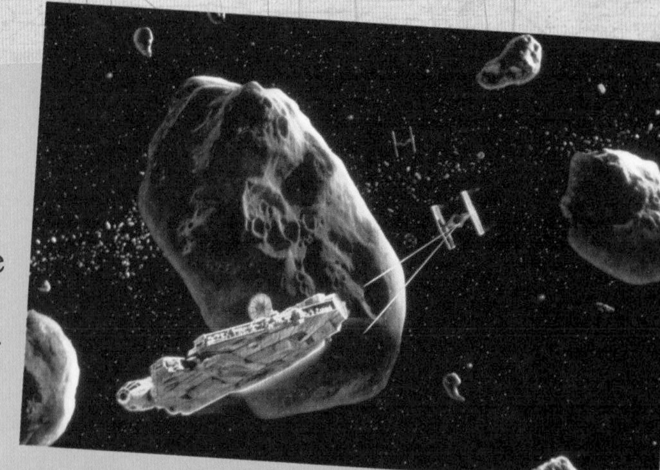

WHAT YOU NEED:

- ✓ Plastic spoon
- ✓ Fine grit sandpaper
- ✓ Honey-brown paint
- ✓ Felt: cream and gray
- ✓ 2 large googly eyes
- ✓ Black marker
- ✓ Hot glue gun

Plastic Spoon Admiral Ackbar

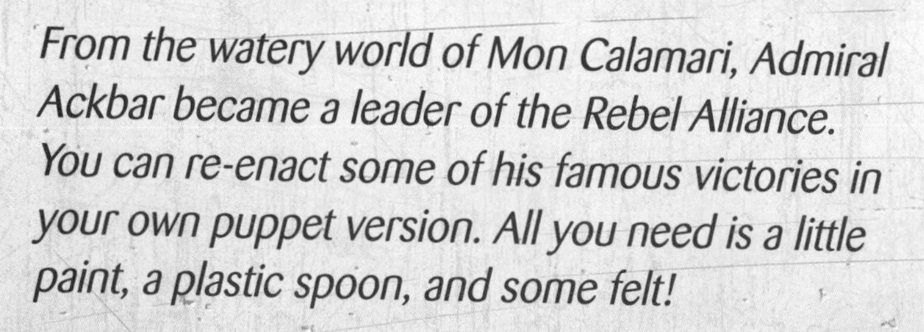

From the watery world of Mon Calamari, Admiral Ackbar became a leader of the Rebel Alliance. You can re-enact some of his famous victories in your own puppet version. All you need is a little paint, a plastic spoon, and some felt!

1 Lightly sand the back of the spoon to knock the shine off.

2 Paint the back of the spoon and the neck (not the handle) with honey-brown paint and set aside to dry.

3 Cut a 7½ cm x 12½ cm triangle from cream felt.

4 Lay the 7½ cm side of the triangle along the neck of the spoon, then trim off the tip off the triangle, exposing about 2½ cm of the handle of the spoon. Use scissors to round the corners. Cut a half circle for the neck of the shirt. Glue the felt to the spoon.

5 From cream felt, cut a collar and glue it to the neck of the shirt.

6 Cut two small squares from gray felt and glue to the upper right corner of the shirt. Glue googly eyes to the lower left and right sides of the spoon and use a marker to add a nose and mouth.

WHAT YOU NEED:

- ✓ Paper towel tube
- ✓ Scissors
- ✓ Silver craft paint
- ✓ Hot glue gun
- ✓ Small cereal box
- ✓ White and brown construction paper
- ✓ Black marker
- ✓ Pencil

Cereal Box Tusken Raider

The Sand People, or Tusken Raiders, covered themselves in desert-colored clothing to protect their skin from the harsh Tatooine desert sun. They covered their eyes with goggles as protection from the sun and wore protective masks with pipes and a mouthpiece that allowed them to breathe. You can outfit your own Tusken Raider using construction paper and a cereal box!

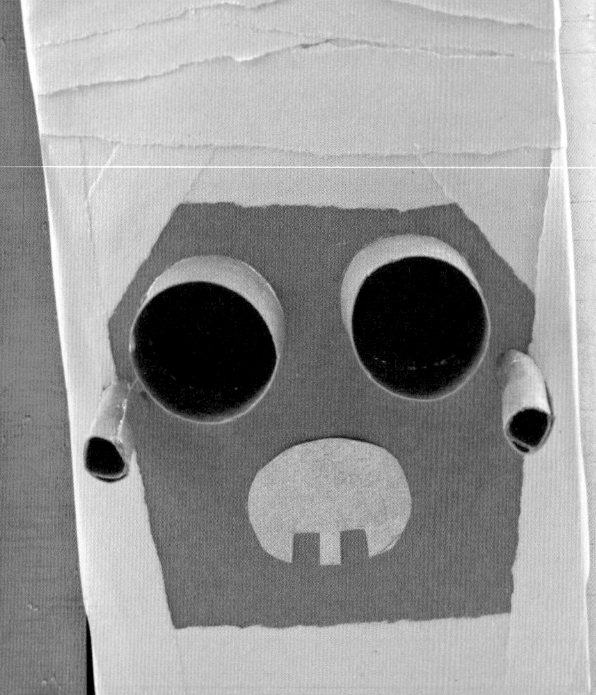

1 Cut an 8 cm piece from the paper towel tube, then cut that in half to create two 4 cm tubes. Paint both of them, inside and out, with silver paint and set aside to dry.

2 From the remaining paper towel tube, cut another section 6 cm long. Cut that tube in half lengthwise to create two half-tubes.

3 Roll up each half-tube and glue it with the hot glue gun to secure. Paint these tubes silver and let them dry.

4 Cut another 4 cm tube from the paper towel tube. As in step 2, cut it in half lengthwise, then cut each of those in half lengthwise. Roll them all up and secure with glue, then paint them in silver.

5 Glue brown paper to the front of the cereal box.

6 Tear white construction paper in strips and glue onto the cereal box, covering the edges of the brown paper, overlapping strips, and wrapping them around the sides and top of the box as shown, leaving the center clear.

7 Use one of the 4 cm silver tubes and a pencil to trace circles onto the brown paper for the eyes. Use a black marker to color in those circles. Glue the silver tubes over the black circles.

8 Glue the long silver tubes to the sides of the face below the eyes.

9 Glue the short silver tubes to the top of the head.

10 From the remaining paper towel tube, cut an oval and cut two square notches from the bottom of the oval. Paint it silver and glue it in place for the mouth.

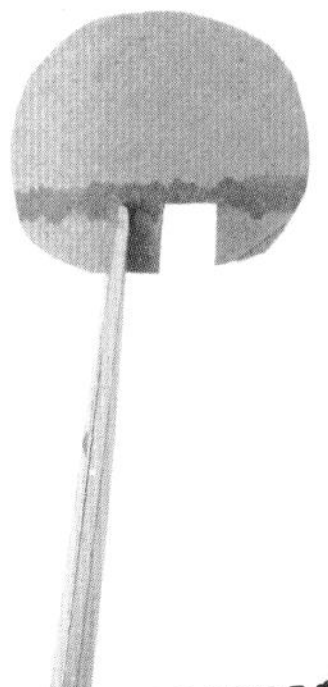

FUN FACT:

"A long time ago in a galaxy far, far away…" These are the words that open the *Star Wars* films.

Foam Cup Greedo

Smelly and rude, Greedo aspired to become a top bounty hunter but really wasn't up to the job. One job your Greedo is up to, though, is storing treasures in your room. And if you're having a Star Wars party, a foam-cup Greedo, lined with tissue paper, is a great way to send home treats!

WHAT YOU NEED

- ✓ 250 ml foam cup
- ✓ Turquoise and purple paint
- ✓ Two 5 cm square pieces of cardboard
- ✓ Scissors
- ✓ 2 cm foam spouncer (round sponge applicator)
- ✓ Craft knife
- ✓ 2 turquoise or light blue pipe cleaners
- ✓ Hot glue gun
- ✓ Black marker

1 Paint the outside and halfway down the inside of the cup with turquoise; set it aside to dry.

2 Cut cardboard into ears and paint both sides turquoise; set aside to dry.

3 Use a foam spouncer to add eyes to the foam cup by dipping in purple paint and applying in a circular motion.

4 Cut slits on the sides of the cup using a craft knife and insert the ears.

5 About 7½ cm from the end of the pipe cleaner, bend upwards and twist.

6 Wrap the other end of the pipe cleaner around the tip of your finger to create a circle shape. Continue until you reach the bent piece.

7 Bend the second pipe cleaner the same way, then twist the two ends together, combining them.

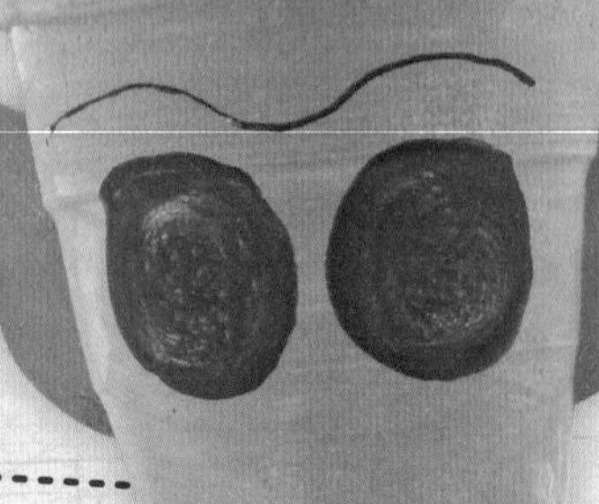

8 Hot glue the pipe cleaners inside the front of the cup behind the eyes.

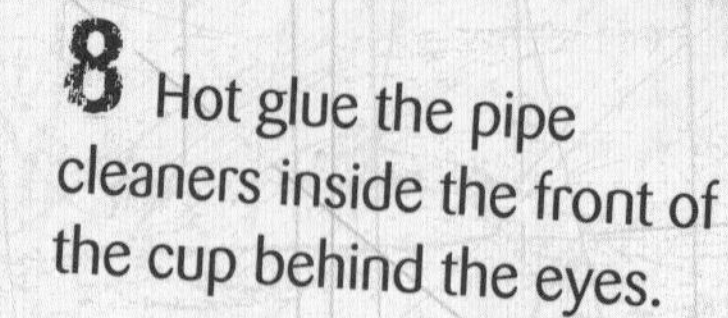

9 Use a black marker to add the mouth and eyebrows.

Flying Death Star

WHAT YOU NEED:

- ✓ 2 white paper plates
- ✓ Pencil
- ✓ Craft knife or scissors
- ✓ Crayons: light gray and yellow or gold
- ✓ Hot glue gun or tape

Wing your very own Death Star through space...well, through the living room, anyway! All you need are a couple of paper plates and some crayons!

1 Outline a 5 cm-diameter hole in the center of each paper plate. You can trace around a cup or glass of the right size. Use a craft knife to cut out the circles.

2 Turn one of the paper plates upside down and begin drawing rectangles to the left and right of the center circle. Continue drawing rectangles until the plate is covered.

3 Color in the rectangles with light gray crayon.

4 Use yellow or gold crayon to add random dashes on the gray rectangles.

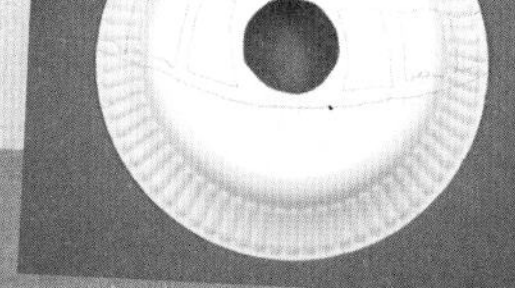

5 Glue or tape the paper plates together at the rims so that the bottom of each plate is facing out.

USE THE FORCE!

Don't have a craft knife? Use the pointy ends of your scissors to poke a hole inside your circle, then wiggle the scissors in so you can cut it out.

Test your aerodynamics by making Death Stars with bigger holes, with smaller holes, some with holes on only one side... which one flies the best?

AT-AT Walker Marionette

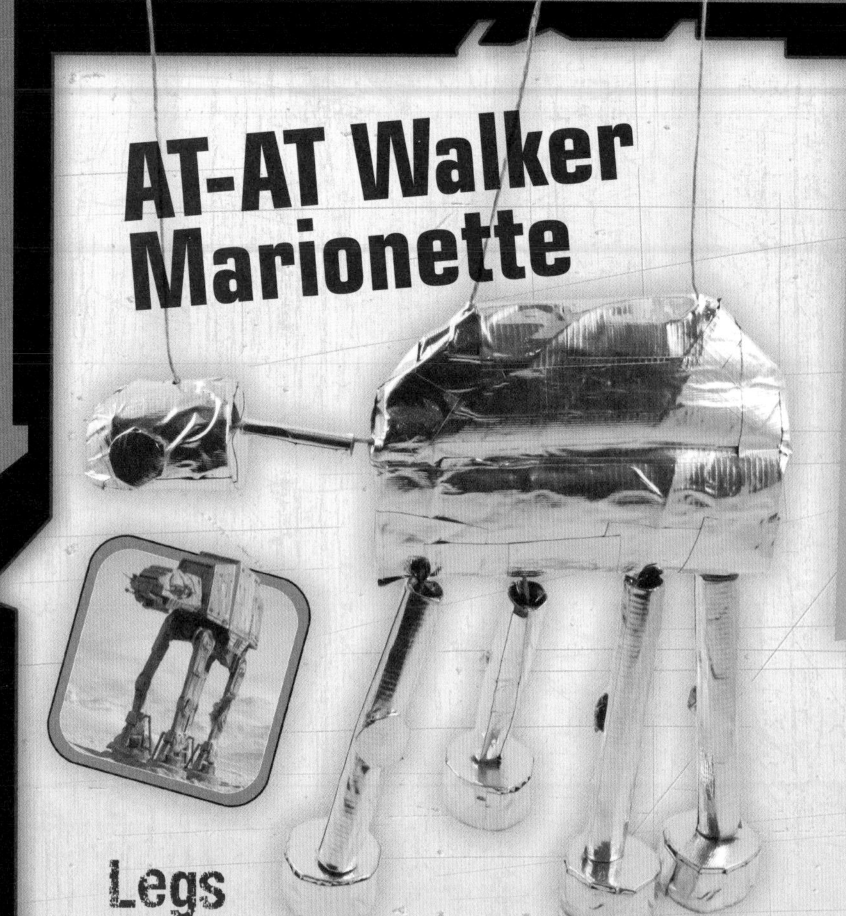

WHAT YOU NEED:

- ✓ Three 28 cm cardboard paper towel rolls
- ✓ Scissors
- ✓ Silver and black duct tape
- ✓ Twine, yarn, or heavy string
- ✓ Drinking straw
- ✓ Paint stir stick or wooden dowel

Create your very own marionette and stomp your way through the ice planet Hoth. You only need a few supplies!

Legs & Feet

1 Cut off a 10 cm-long piece from one cardboard tube. Cut that piece into four 2½ cm pieces. These will be the feet. Set the remaining tube aside.

2 Cover one of the open ends of each of the four pieces with silver duct tape.

3 Use the point of the scissors to poke a hole in the center of the tape on each foot.

4 Measure and cut four 43 cm-long pieces of twine. Insert one end of the twine into the hole in the foot and tie in a knot on the inside, as shown. Repeat for remaining three feet.

5 Cover the feet completely with silver duct tape.

6 Cut the second cardboard tube in half so that you have two 14 cm pieces. Cut both of those pieces in half lengthwise.

7 Roll each one into a slender tube and secure with tape. Completely cover the tubes in silver tape. These are the legs.

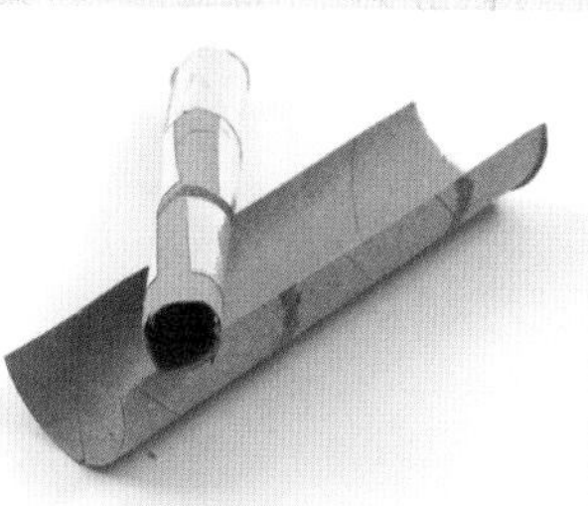

8 Cut a 2½ cm piece from another cardboard tube, and cut that piece open. Draw five circles—you can trace around a ten-cent coin—and cut them out.

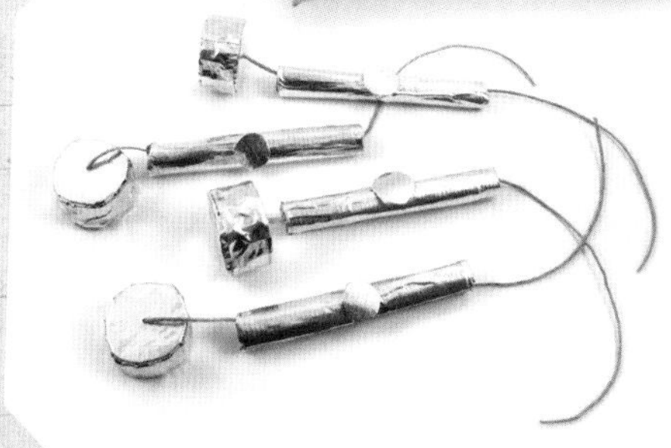

9 Cover the circles with silver tape. Roll small pieces of tape, sticky side out, to attach the circles. Stick four to the knees using rolled-up pieces of tape. Save the last one for the head.

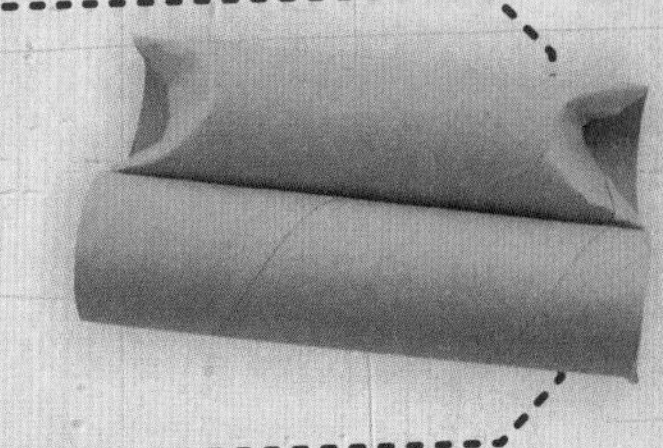

10 Thread the string from the foot through the leg tube and set legs aside.

Body

1 Find the tube you set aside in step 1 when you were working on the legs. This tube should be 18 cm long. Cut another 18 cm tube from the last cardboard tube. Now you have two 18 cm tubes.

2 Set aside the remaining 4 cm piece.

3 Use your fingers to dent the ends of one of the 18 cm body tubes.

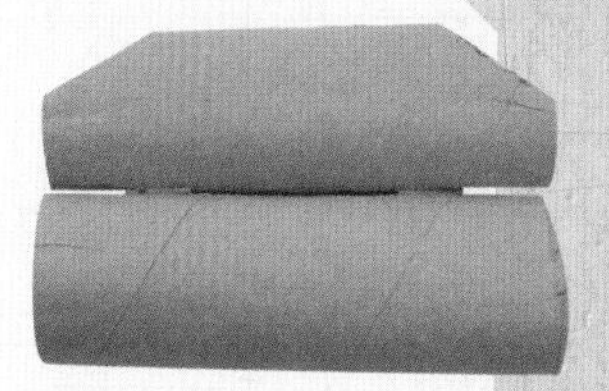

4 Turn the tube sideways so that the dents are at the top, and attach the two body tubes together with a little tape. You can either roll the tape or tape around the outside of the tubes. Squash the tubes flat with your hands, which will make the body appear larger.

Head

1 Trim 2½ cm from the remaining 10 cm tube. Cut five 2½ cm slits in the end of the 7½ cm tube.

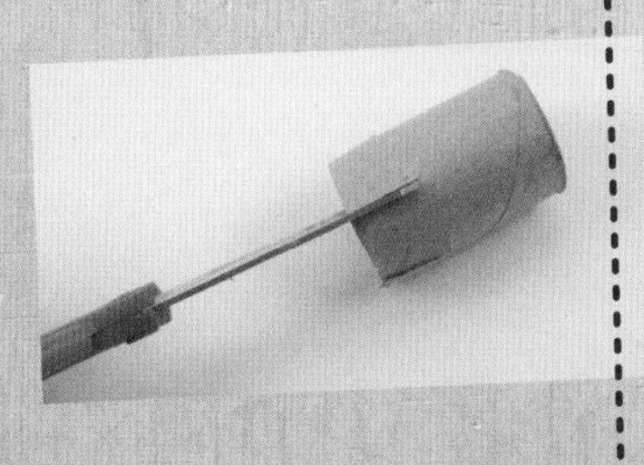

2 Fold the slits inward and secure with silver tape to create the "nose."

Assembly

1 Lay the body on the table. Tape the twine from two legs to one side of the body, and tape the twine from the other two legs to the other side of the body. Trim off the excess twine.

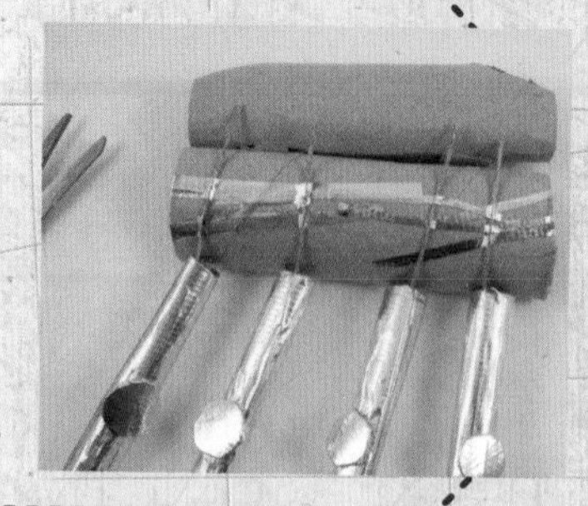

2 Measure and cut a 90 cm piece of twine and thread it through the top (dented) body tube. Pull it through the other end and secure it to the top of the tail end of the body tube with tape. This is the "head" string.

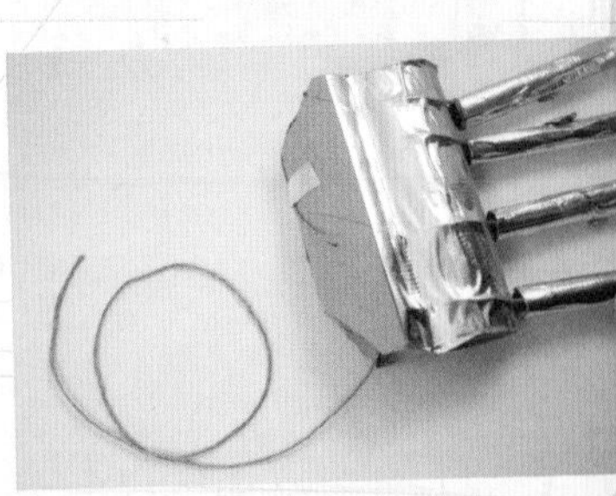

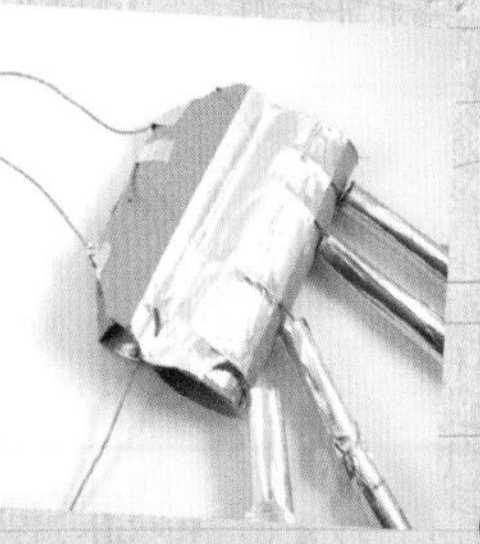

3 Measure and cut a 120 cm piece of twine and thread it through the top body tube as well, matching up the ends of the string to ensure the lengths are the same. Secure it to the body tube by taping to the "dents." This is the "body" string.

4 Cut a 5 cm piece from the drinking straw and thread the head string through it.

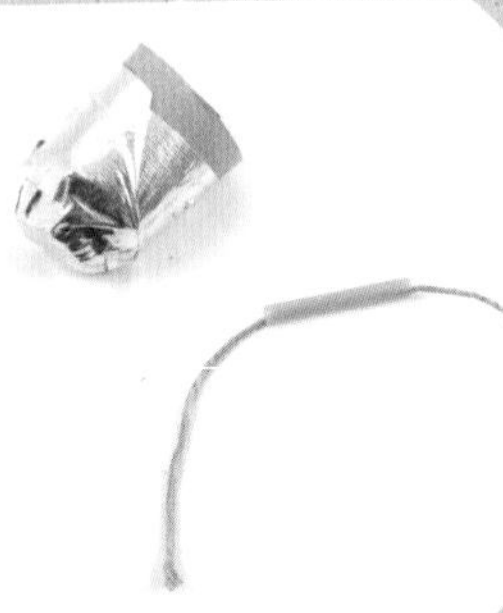

5 Poke a hole in the top of the head and thread the head string up through the inside of the head.

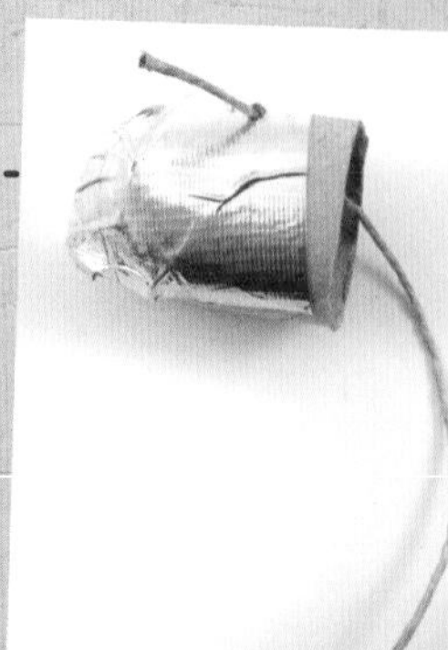

6 Cover the straw with silver tape.

7 Cover the rest of the head with silver tape, leaving just a little space between the head and the straw. Attach the remaining cardboard circle you made in steps 8–9 of the legs.

8 Cover any remaining exposed cardboard with pieces of silver tape.

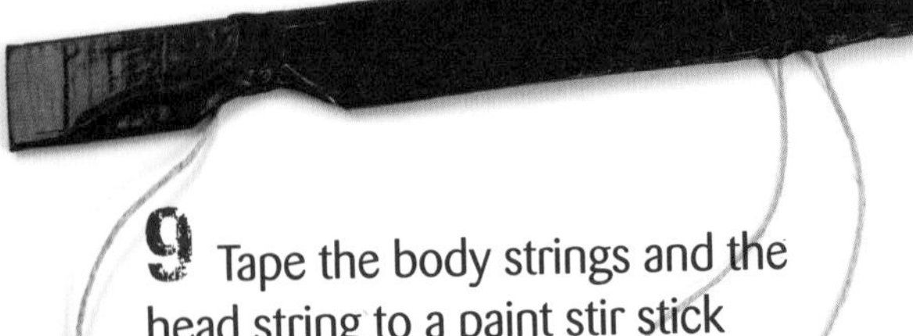

9 Tape the body strings and the head string to a paint stir stick to use as your handle. Cover the stir stick with black duct tape.

WHAT YOU NEED:

- ✓ Wooden clothespin
- ✓ Tracing paper
- ✓ Pencil
- ✓ Brown construction paper
- ✓ Scissors
- ✓ Hot glue gun or quick drying craft glue
- ✓ Small googly eye
- ✓ Brown marker

TEMPLATE

TEMPLATE

Clothespin Jar Jar Binks

He might have been clumsy, but Jar Jar Binks always had good intentions, and he led his people in the fight to save their planet, Naboo. You can make a simple Jar Jar puppet from a clothespin and some construction paper. Practice his unforgettable voice while you're working and you'll be ready in minutes.

1 Trace the Jar Jar shapes onto tracing paper or thin white copier paper. Cut these shapes out and trace around them on brown construction paper. Cut these shapes out.

2 Glue the shapes to the clothespin, with the bigger shape on the top as shown.

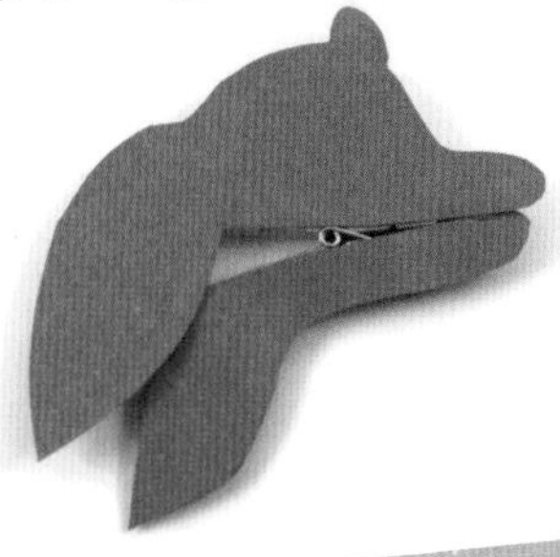

3 Glue on a googly eye on the top of the head.

4 Use a brown marker to add his nose and lines down the back of his neck and ear.

5 Squeeze and release the clothespin to open and close Jar Jar's mouth.

Darth Vader Paper Bag Puppet

Practice your best Darth Vader voice while you're making this paper bag puppet. Don't forget the noisy breathing! Here's a good line to try: "You underestimate the power of the dark side." Scary, right?

WHAT YOU NEED:

- ✓ Paper lunch bag
- ✓ Black and silver acrylic craft paint
- ✓ Paintbrush
- ✓ Construction paper: black, red, blue, brown
- ✓ Silver crayon
- ✓ Scissors
- ✓ Glue stick
- ✓ Small (15 cm) paper plate

1 Paint the paper bag black and stand it up on the open end to allow it to dry.

2 Paint a 10 cm-square piece of construction paper (any color) with silver paint and let dry.

3 Paint a piece of black construction paper with black paint and let dry.

Breastplate

1 Measure and cut a 13 cm x 5 cm rectangle from black paper.

2 Cut the bottom into a curved shape as shown. Cut strips from the silver-painted paper and glue them to the breastplate.

3 Glue the breastplate onto the standing-up bag about 2½ cm from the top.

Light Panel

1 Measure and cut a 6 cm x 5 cm black rectangle.

2 Cut small rectangles from red, blue, and silver paper and glue them to the black rectangle.

3 Glue this light panel to the paper bag about 1 cm below the breastplate.

Belt

1 Measure and cut a 13 cm x 2½ cm black rectangle.

2 Cut a circle from silver paper about the size of a ten cent coin and glue it to the center of the belt.

3 Cut small rectangles from blue, red, and silver paper and glue to the belt.

4 Glue the belt to the paper bag below the light panel.

Cape

1 Fold a sheet of black or dark brown construction paper in half so the short ends meet. Fold in half again.

2 Open the second fold. Starting from the bottom corner of the open end, cut on a curved diagonal up to the first fold, as shown.

3 Open the paper cape and glue to the back of the bag.

Helmet & Face

1 Trace a small paper plate (a dessert plate) onto the painted black construction paper.

2 Cut around the top half of your circle, then straight down the sides to create a dome shape.

3 Cut a triangle with 5 cm sides and a 9 cm base from black paper.

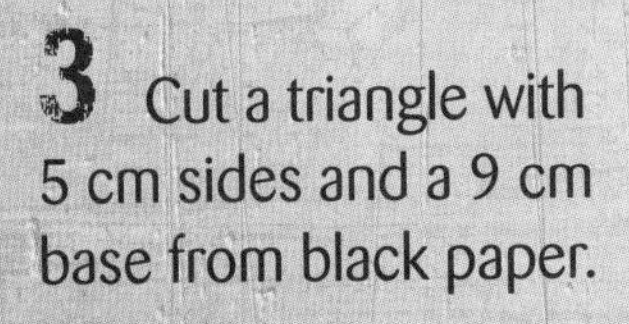

4 Use a silver crayon to draw stripes on the triangle.

5 Glue the base of the triangle onto the very top of the bag. This is the mouthpiece.

6 Using the template, cut two eyebrows and one nosepiece from dark brown construction paper. Glue the nosepiece above the mouthpiece.

7 Position the eyebrows above the nosepiece as shown.

8 Line up the dome helmet and trim if needed, then glue in place on top of the bag. It will stick up beyond the edge of the bag.

Wookiee Finger Puppets

- ✓ Brown felt
- ✓ Scissors
- ✓ Hot glue gun or felt glue
- ✓ Scrap of black felt
- ✓ Small brown pom-pom
- ✓ 2 small googly eyes
- ✓ White paint
- ✓ Toothpick

Here's a secret. Although they can look pretty scary, Wookiees are actually pretty gentle creatures–with their friends, anyway. But don't provoke them, because they can get very snarly!

1 Measure a strip of felt the length of your finger and the width of two of your fingers. Cut it out.

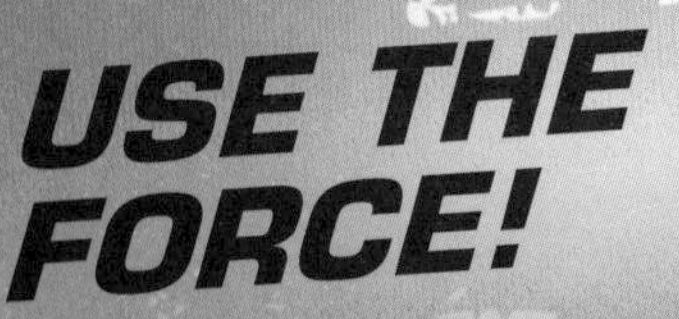

Use a crayon or chalk to mark your measurements onto the felt.

If you want to make a happy Wookiee, make a little smile from the black felt.

2 Run some glue along the edges of the felt, then fold in half to make a finger puppet body.

3 Use scissors to cut long, thin triangles in the bottom of the puppet, to get that shaggy look.

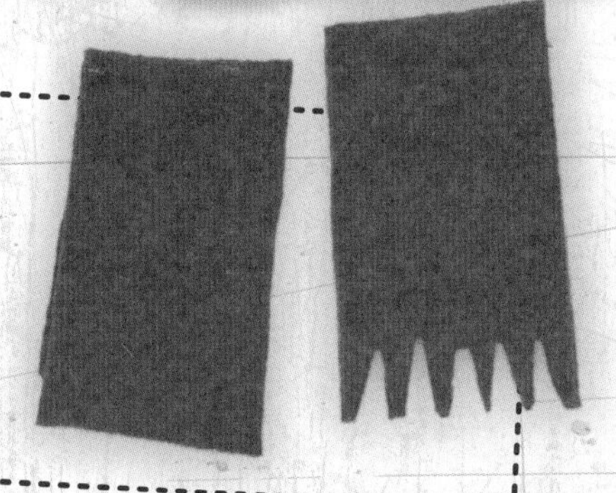

4 Cut a small oval from black felt and glue to the center of the puppet.

5 Glue a brown pom-pom directly above the black oval for a nose.

6 Glue googly eyes above the pom-pom.

7 Cut two eyebrows from blown felt and glue in place.

8 Use a toothpick dipped in white paint to add teeth to the black oval.

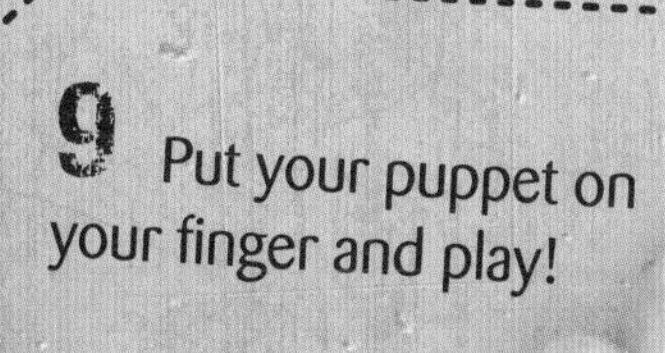

9 Put your puppet on your finger and play!

FUN FACT:

Wookiees are from the planet Kashyyyk. In their own language, they call themselves the People of the Trees, and they live in tree houses perched high in their native forests. Big and tall with shaggy hair, they look fierce—and have terrible tempers—but they usually are kind and very, very loyal to their friends.

Jawa Hand Puppet

Jawas always travel in crowds... You and your friends can make an entire colony of Jawa hand puppets in the morning, and host a puppet show in the afternoon!

WHAT YOU NEED:

- ✓ 2 sheets brown felt for each puppet
- ✓ Knit glove or your hand for tracing
- ✓ Yellow or white crayon or chalk
- ✓ Hot glue gun or needle and thread
- ✓ Felt scraps: black, yellow, tan
- ✓ Scissors

1 Use chalk or a crayon to trace around your hand or a glove onto the brown felt, tracing the thumb and pinky individually then making one section for the remaining fingers. Be sure to trace around 1-2½ cm larger than the actual glove or 4-5 cm wider than your hand.

USE THE FORCE!

There are two measures for the extra margin you need to add when you're measuring for your puppet. If you're gluing, add the higher amount for the seam allowance so that the puppet glove is not too small when you turn it inside out. Glue will take up more of the seam allowance.

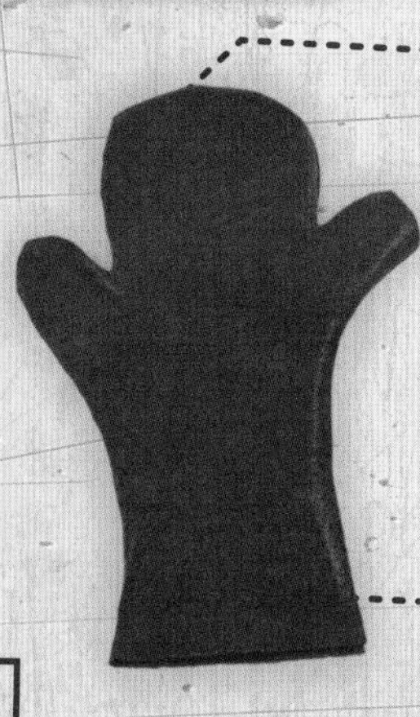

2 Cutting through both sheets of felt at the same time, cut out the puppet shape.

3 Glue or sew the puppet pieces together, leaving the wrist end open. Let the glue dry completely.

4 Turn the puppet inside out so your seam is inside.

5 Cut an oval from black felt small enough to fit on the face of the puppet and glue in place.

6 Cut two small rectangles from yellow felt and glue to the black felt, to make gleaming eyes.

7 Cut a strip of tan felt for the bandolier. Cut squares from brown felt and glue to the bandolier. Glue the bandolier to the puppet, over one shoulder.

FUN FACT:

Did you know that R2-D2 and C-3PO were once captured by Jawas? They were on Princess Leia's ship when it was captured by stormtroopers. The two escaped, but their pod crash-landed on Tatooine. There they were seized by a band of Jawas. The Jawas sold them to Luke Skywalker's family, and the rest is *Star Wars* history!

Duct Tape Lightsabers

Every Jedi Knight has mastered the use of the lightsaber—a weapon that relies on a beam of pure energy controlled by the Force. You can prepare for your very own intergalactic battle—all you need to get ready is some duct tape and wrapping paper tubes!

WHAT YOU NEED:

- ✓ Cardboard tubes from wrapping paper
- ✓ Duct tape: red, blue, silver, black
- ✓ Craft knife
- ✓ Cutting mat

1 Cover a tube with red (or blue) duct tape. Three strips running down the length of the tube should do it. Tuck the excess inside the end of the tube.

2 Measure and cut three 23 cm strips of silver tape for the handle. Cover 20 cm of the end of the tube, tucking the extra 3 cm inside the end. Repeat with the remaining two strips to complete the handle.

3 Measure and cut three 10 cm strips of black tape. Cut each of these strips into four thin strips, for a total of twelve strips. Attach thin strips to the silver handle as the "grips."

WHAT YOU NEED:

- ✓ Paint stir stick
- ✓ Brown faux fur
- ✓ Scissors
- ✓ Hot glue gun
- ✓ Dark brown felt
- ✓ Gray felt
- ✓ Medium brown pom-pom
- ✓ 2 googly eyes

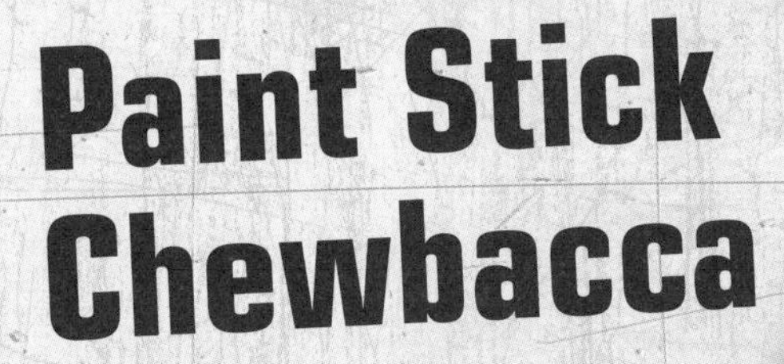

Paint Stick Chewbacca

Make your own Wookiee sidekick with some paint stir sticks and faux fur! Here's how!

1 Here's how to cover the paint stick with faux fur. Turn the fur upside down, and measure the correct length. Glue the stick to the back of the fur at one end, then add some more glue next to the stick, fold, and trim.

2 Cut two 13 cm x 1 cm strips from the remaining fur for arms. Glue arms to the back of the stick. The furry side will face toward the front.

3 Cut a strip 23 cm x 1 cm of dark brown felt for the bandolier.

4 Cut five or six squares and rectangles from gray felt for the ammo boxes.

5 Glue the ammo boxes onto the bandolier toward the middle of the strip. Once the glue is dry, glue the ends of the bandolier together. Place the bandolier over the top of the paint stick, over one arm and under the other. Glue it in place.

6 Use glue to attach a pom-pom nose and googly eyes.

USE THE FORCE!

Many hardware stores give out paint stir sticks every time you buy a can of paint. If you don't have extras at home, ask nicely in the store and they'll probably give you a few.

WHAT YOU NEED:

- ✓ 1 sheet white paper
- ✓ Pencil
- ✓ Ruler
- ✓ Scissors
- ✓ 4 white paper plates
- ✓ Black, gray, and light blue markers
- ✓ Hot glue gun

Paper Plate Millennium Falcon

Han Solo and Chewbacca piloted the full-size version of the Millennium Falcon*, but now you can create your own play-size version with a few paper plates!*

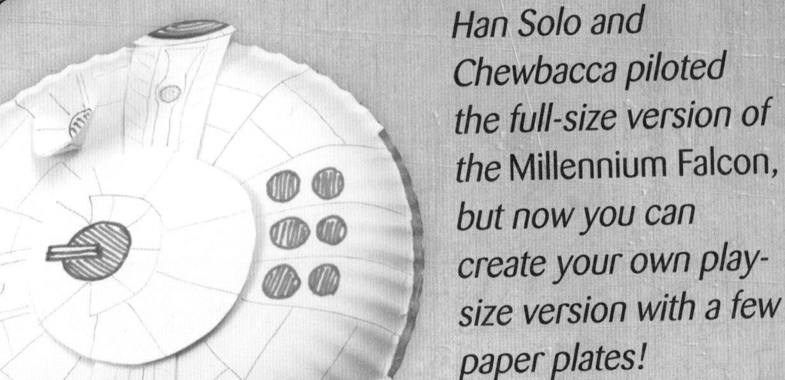

Mandibles

1 On white paper, draw a 13 cm-long line with a pencil. At the end draw a 2 cm line at a 90-degree angle to the right. Working downward, draw a 10 cm long line slightly slanted away from your first line. This will be your template for the mandibles.

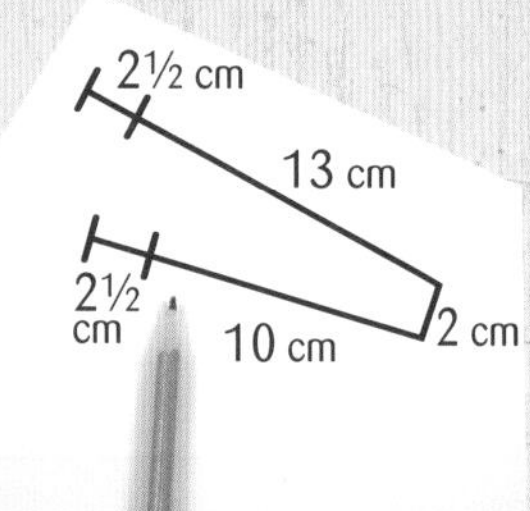

2 Cut out your template, adding 2½ cm to the wide end to allow room for the mandible to be glued inside.

3 Cut one paper plate in half. Line up your tail templates along the straight edges and cut them both from the plate.

Antenna

1 From another paper plate, cut out the center circle (keep the outer ring for later). Cut a smaller circle from that, about 5 cm in diameter.

2 Draw a small circle in the center and lines going from the circle to the outer edge, like sunrays.

3 Cut slits on both sides up to the center circle. To make the circle three-dimensional, tuck one side of the slit behind the other and hot-glue in place. Repeat for the second slit.

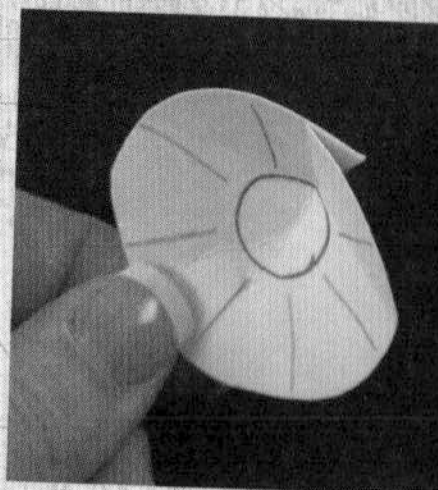

Cockpit

1 To make the cockpit, cut two pieces from the ring left from making the antenna. One piece is around 7½ cm x 7½ cm and the other around 5 cm x 10 cm.

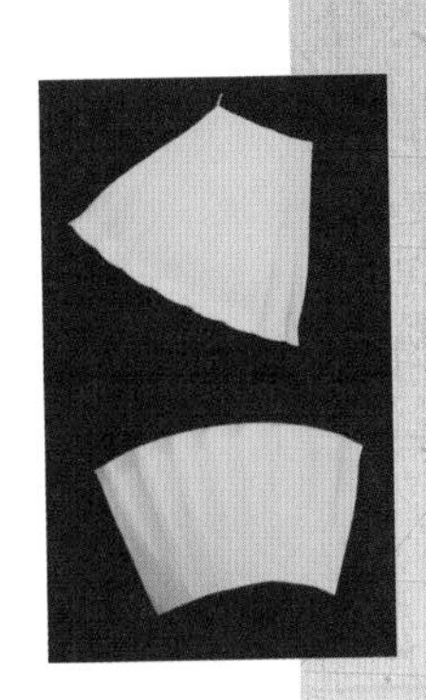

2 On the 5 cm x 10 cm piece, draw black lines for the cockpit windows.

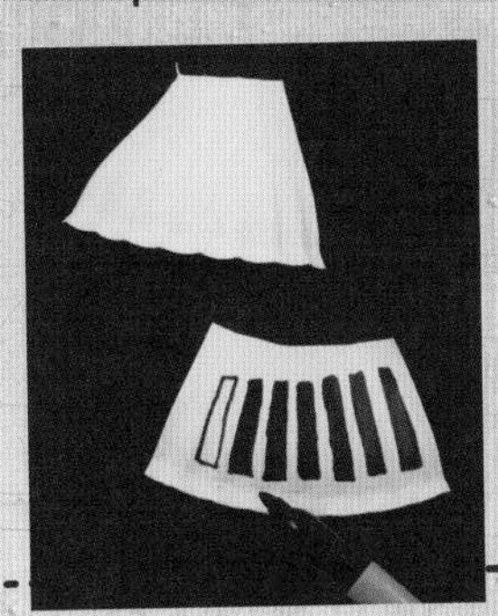

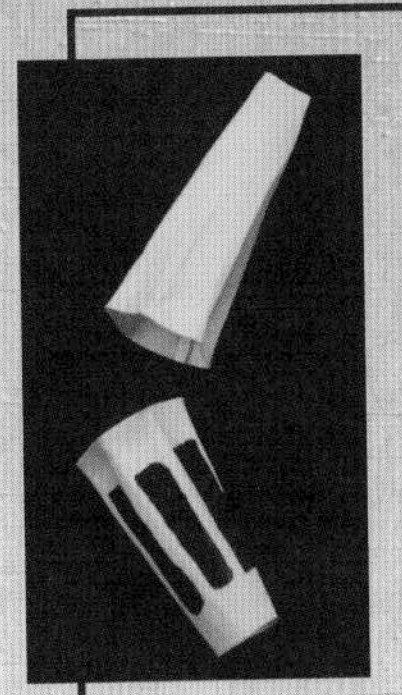

3 Roll up each piece, making sure the 7½ cm x 7½ cm piece will tuck inside the 5 cm x 10 cm piece, then secure with glue.

Assemble your *Millennium Falcon*!

1 Place a third paper plate on the work surface and hot glue the mandibles, side by side, to the edge of the plate.

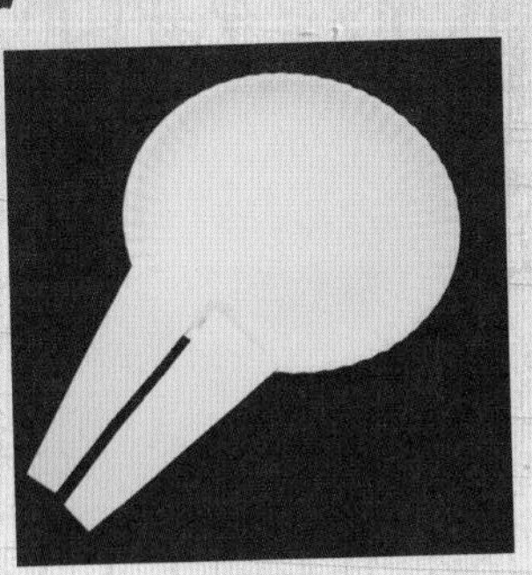

2 Place the fourth paper plate over the top and glue the plates together, rim to rim.

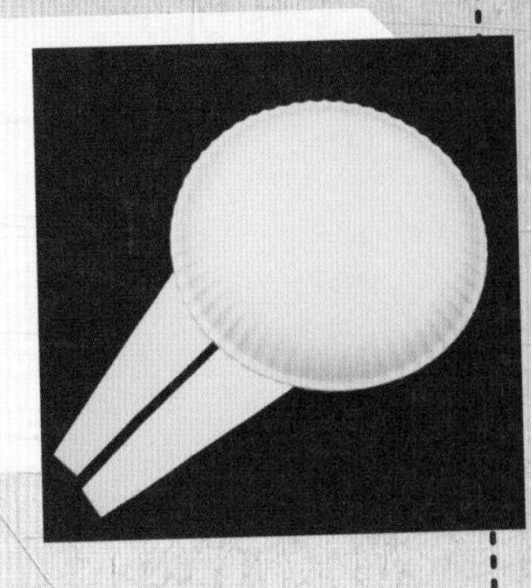

3 From some scraps, cut two strips to place across the top of the "ship," and glue two ovals to the ends of each strip to create the escape pods.

4 Cut a circle from a scrap plate and glue it on top of the escape pods in the middle.

5 Glue the antenna and cockpit in place.

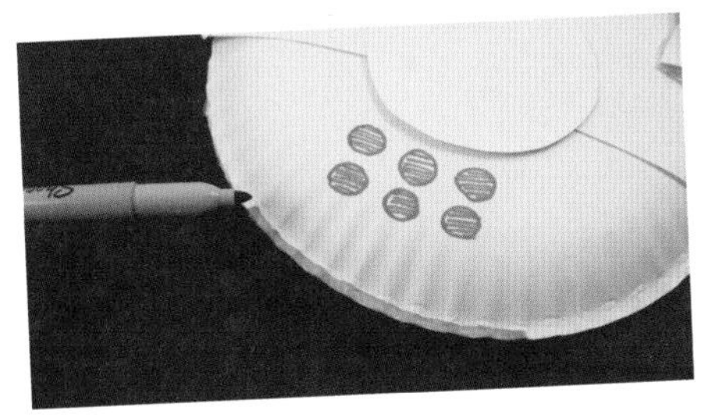

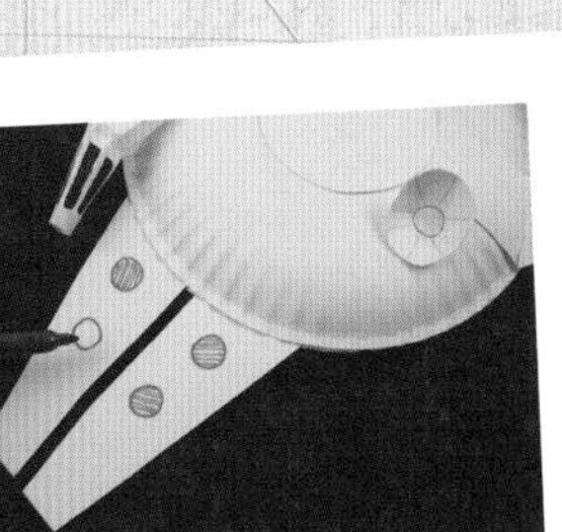

6 Add details to the mandibles and the rest of the ship using markers and pencil.

Princess Leia Puppet

Be inspired by the bravery and smarts of Princess Leia with this stick puppet in your hand. This can also be used as a bookmark! A great addition to your desk or school supplies.

WHAT YOU NEED:

- ✓ 15 cm jumbo craft stick
- ✓ Paint: white, peach, brown, pink, black, silver
- ✓ Paintbrushes
- ✓ Red marker
- ✓ 2 medium brown pom-poms
- ✓ Scissors
- ✓ Hot glue gun

1 Measure 11½ cm from one end of the jumbo craft stick. Paint the longer section white on both sides. Paint the other part peach, just on the front.

2 Dip a paintbrush in pink paint, then apply the brush to a cloth or paper towel, moving it in circles to remove most of the paint. Dab the dried brush gently on the peach section of the craft stick to create the rosy cheeks.

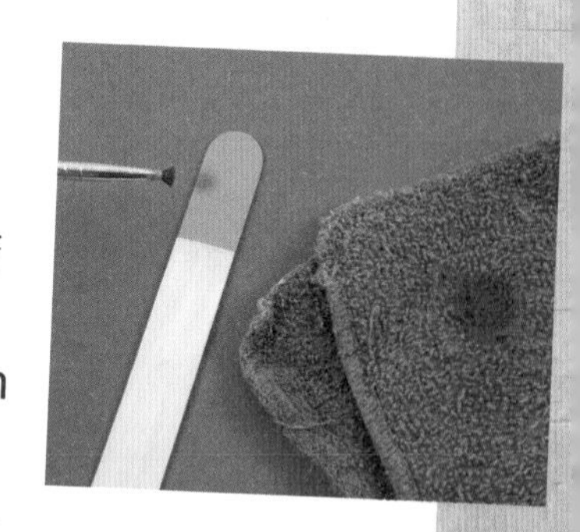

3 Use a red marker to draw a mouth. Dip the handle end of your paintbrush into white paint to dot on eyes.

4 Paint brown on top of the craft stick and around the back for the princess's hair.

5 Use a thin paintbrush and silver paint to add the necklace and belt.

6 For the necklace charms, dip the handle of the paintbrush into silver paint and dot paint on along the necklace line.

7 Mix a little white and silver paint and dot on the medallions for the belt.

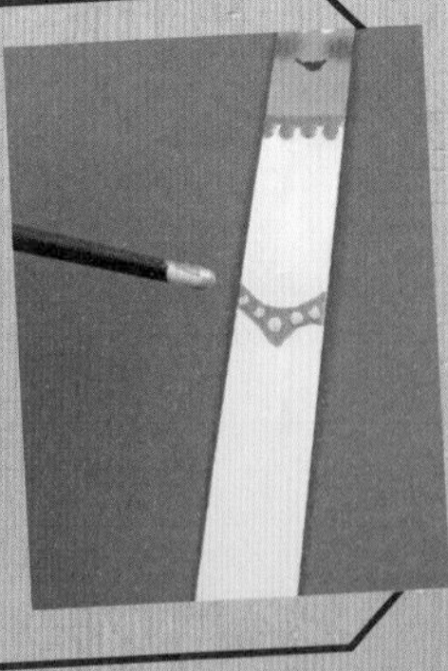

8 Once the eyes and hair are dry, use a toothpick to add the pupils with black paint.

9 To make Princess Leia's famous hairstyle, trim one side of one of the pom-poms to make it slightly flatter, then glue to the side of the head. Repeat with the second pom-pom.

"May the Force Be with You" Scratch Art

Scratch art is a great way to create something fun to hang on your bedroom wall. Use this classic method to remind you of the Force within you!

WHAT YOU NEED:

- ✓ White construction paper
- ✓ Crayons in several bright colors
- ✓ Black acrylic craft paint
- ✓ Paintbrush
- ✓ Ruler
- ✓ Pencil
- ✓ Wooden skewer

1 Use crayons to color the construction paper with several blocks of bright colors. Press firmly with the crayons to get a thick coat, and don't leave any white areas.

2 Once the paper is completely colored in, paint over the colored surface with a generous coat of black acrylic paint. Set aside to dry completely.

MAY THE FORCE BE WITH YOU

3 Use a ruler as a guide if you want your words to be straight on your paper. You can write the words lightly in pencil first, or simply freehand it!

4 Use the skewer to carefully scrape off the top layer of paint, revealing the color underneath. Press firmly but carefully so you don't tear the paper.

WHAT YOU NEED:

- ✓ White sand
- ✓ 3 small bowls
- ✓ Red and blue food coloring
- ✓ Paintbrush
- ✓ White craft glue
- ✓ 2 pieces of sandpaper, different grits so that one is darker than the other
- ✓ Scissors
- ✓ White and reddish-orange crayons

Tatooine Desert Sand Art

Luke Skywalker grew up on his uncle's moisture farm on the planet Tatooine before becoming a Jedi. It was a remote and lonely, desertlike place, covered in sand and heated by two strong suns, Tatoo I and Tatoo II. You can create a picture of Luke's home planet using sandpaper and colored sand you make yourself!

1 Pour one tablespoon of white sand into three small bowls.

2 To one of the bowls, add one drop of red food coloring. This will give you pink sand.

3 Add one drop of blue and two drops of red food coloring to another bowl. This will give you purple sand.

4 To the last bowl add one drop of blue food coloring. This will give you blue sand.

5 Stir the food coloring into the sand in each bowl until thoroughly mixed.

6 Use a paintbrush to spread white glue across the top of one of the sheets of sandpaper.

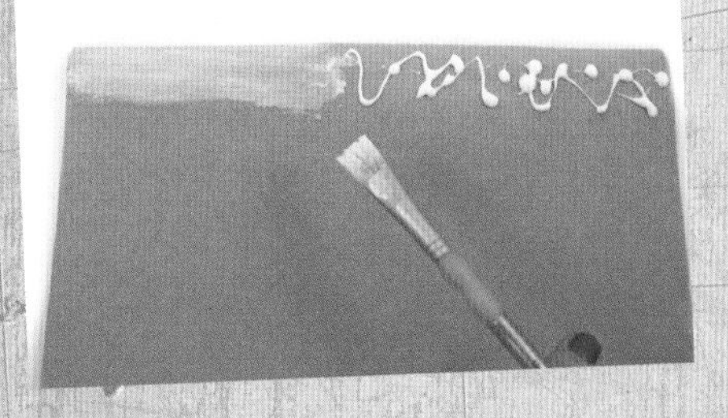

7 Place the sandpaper on a tray and sprinkle pink sand over the glue. Tap off any excess.

8 Paint a second area below the pink with white glue.

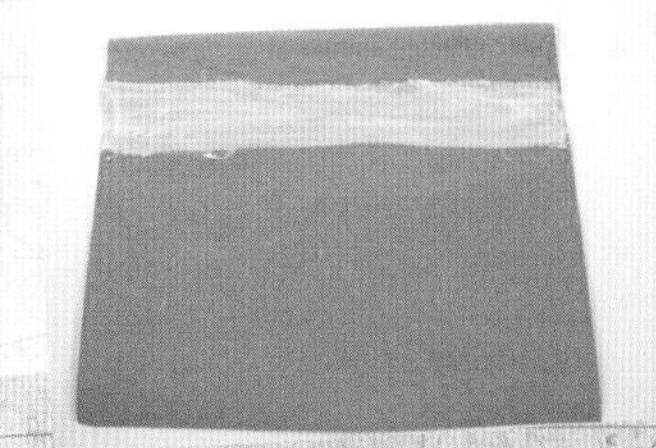

9 Sprinkle with purple sand and tap off any excess.

10 Paint a third area below the purple with white glue and sprinkle with blue sand, tapping off any excess.

11 Use the paintbrush to spread glue in random areas along the bottom half of the sandpaper, then sprinkle with white sand and tap off any excess.

12 From the second sheet of sandpaper, cut a curved rectangular shape from the left side. Cut a smaller rectangle from the right side.

13 Glue these two pieces onto the left side of the first sheet of sandpaper, as shown. This is a traditional Tatooine building, like the one Luke lived in.

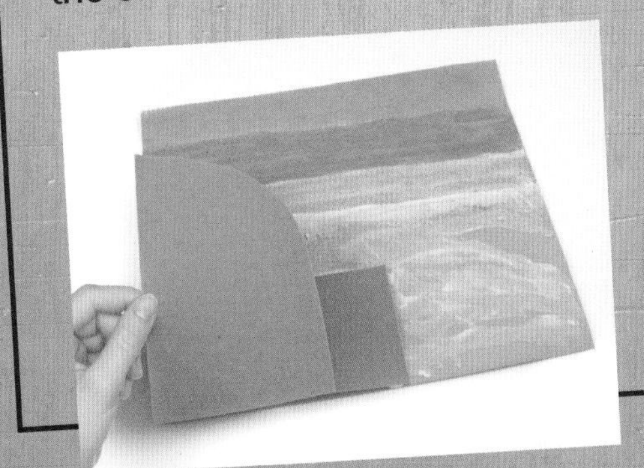

14 Make Tatooine's two suns. Cut two small circles from a scrap of sandpaper, and use crayons to color one white and one reddish-orange. Glue the suns to the sky portion of your sand art.

Emperor Palpatine's Throne Room Diorama

WHAT YOU NEED:

- ✓ Shoe box with attached lid
- ✓ Craft paint: black, gray, white
- ✓ Paper plate
- ✓ Small snack or yoghurt container
- ✓ Toothpick
- ✓ Paintbrush

Turn an old shoe box into a fun diorama that also doubles as storage for your Star Wars action figures! This version is of Emperor Palpatine's throne room on the Death Star, but you could create any scene you like.

1 Paint the inside of the lid gray and the inside of the box black.

USE THE FORCE!

It's a good idea to paint the gray first, because if you paint a little too far into the box, you can easily paint over the gray with the black paint.

2 Mix together four parts gray paint with one part black paint.

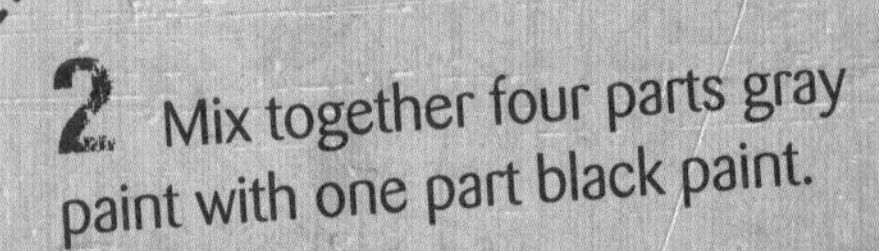

3 Paint the box and the center of the paper plate with the dark gray mixture.

4 Cut out the center of the painted plate.

5 Fold the circle in half. Fold it in half again and in half a third time until you have a skinny wedge.

6 When you unfold the circle, the fold marks will outline triangles. Fold the circle in half again, so your fold falls in the middle of one of the triangles. Use scissors to cut out the center. Repeat until all eight centers have been cut out.

7 The cut-out circle is going to be the viewing window behind Emperor Palpatine's throne, and the small box will be the platform from which he issues his commands. Glue the circle to the inside of the shoebox and glue the painted box just below it, as shown.

8 Dip a toothpick in white paint and dot stars in the black areas of the circle.

9 Place Emperor Palpatine on the box and his Imperial guards at the bottom. Position the pilots and soldiers ready to protect the Emperor!

FUN FACT:

Emperor Palpatine has throne rooms everywhere he goes, protected by his Royal Guards. They all have large, round windows behind his throne. His main throne room is on Coruscant, in the Galactic Core.

Pasta AT-AT Walker

All Terrain Armored Transport—better known as AT-AT walkers—were used by the Imperial army. Like tanks with legs, they were slow but strong. Believe it or not, you can make your own from dried pasta noodles.

WHAT YOU NEED:

- ✓ 20 cm x 25 cm piece of sturdy cardboard (a cereal box, the back of a writing pad, etc)
- ✓ Large tube pasta (rigatoni)
- ✓ Small tube pasta (ditalini)
- ✓ Wheel pasta (wagon wheels)
- ✓ White craft glue

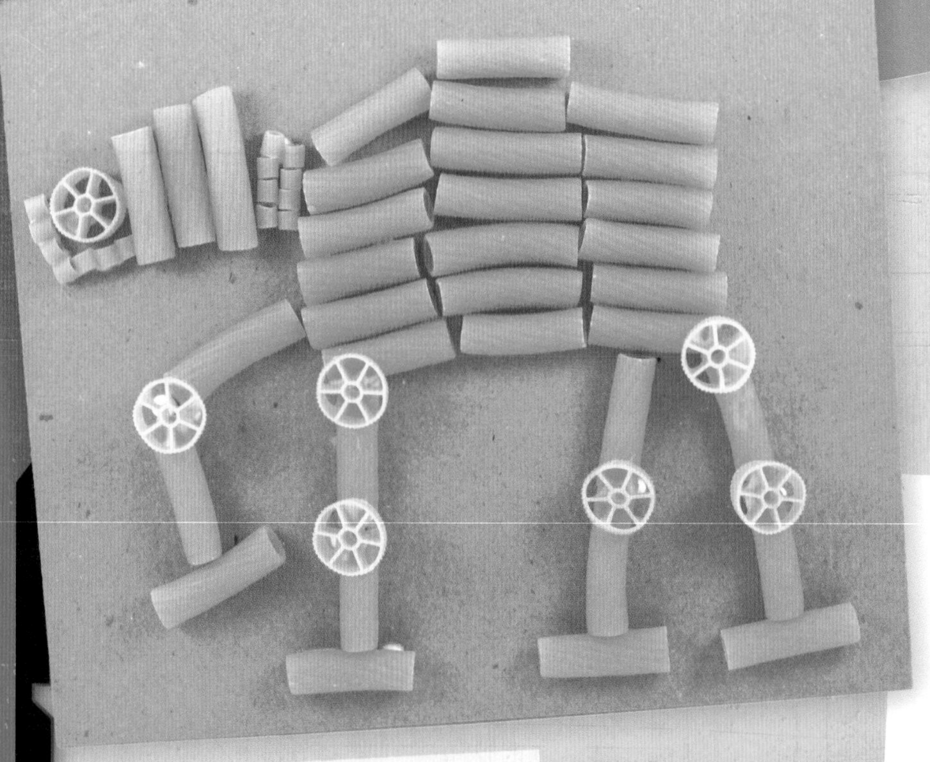

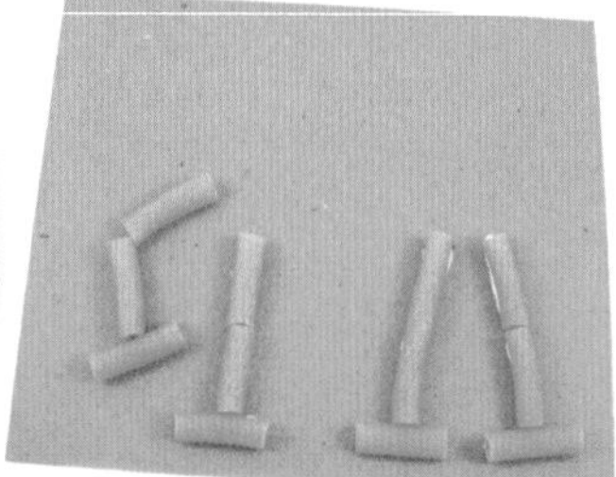

1 Glue three pieces of tube pasta horizontally along the bottom of the cardboard. Use the picture of the completed art as a guide for placement. These will be the back feet and one of the front feet.

2 Glue a fourth tube about 2½ cm above the front horizontal foot and tilt it upward to the right.

3 Glue two pasta tubes vertically above the back horizontal feet for the legs. For the raised tilted foot, glue the first tube vertically then the second at an angle so that the leg appears bent at the knee.

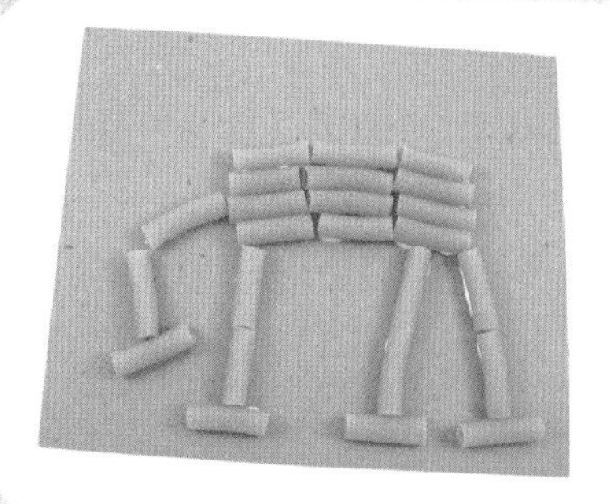

4 Glue three pasta tubes horizontally across the top of the back legs and the straight front leg. Make another row, and another, until you have a total of six rows up to build the body. Glue a single pasta tube on top in the middle.

5 For the neck, glue eight small pasta tubes, in two columns of four small tubes each, coming off the front of the body.

6 Glue three large pasta tubes vertically for the head.

7 Glue a pasta wheel to the front of the pasta head.

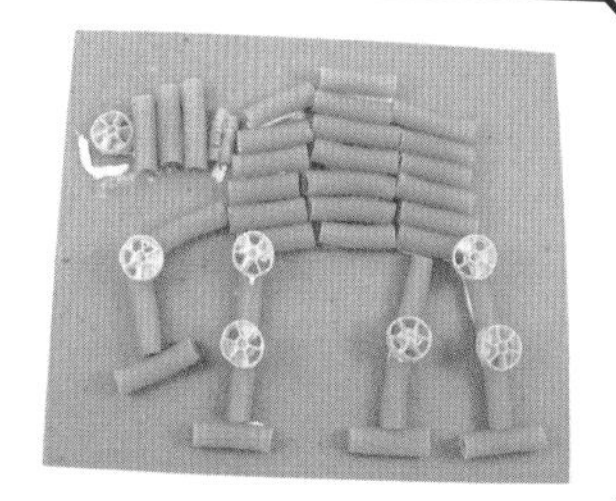

8 Glue small pasta tubes wrapping around the head.

9 Glue a pasta wheel on the joint of each leg and at the top of the last back leg and the second front leg.

FUN FACT:

Heavily armored and heavily armed, AT-AT walkers are more than 15 m high! The "head" holds the command station, and the main body can hold as many as 40 soldiers plus their equipment.

Glow-in-the-Dark Word Board

Let the daylight or your lamp charge your word board, then enjoy its glow when you go to bed at night! Once you get started, you can create lots of art for your room, using famous phrases from your favorite Star Wars *scenes.*

WHAT YOU NEED:

- ✓ 20 cm x 25½ cm canvas
- ✓ Black and white craft paint
- ✓ Paintbrush
- ✓ Old toothbrush
- ✓ Glow-in-the-dark fabric paint pen

1 Paint the canvas black. Let dry.

2 Dip the toothbrush in water and dab off any excess water on a paper towel. Dip the damp toothbrush in white paint and press the bristles into a paper towel to remove excess paint.

3 Hold the toothbrush over the canvas and drag your finger across the bristles of the toothbrush to create a starry splatter effect. Continue until you have lots of stars! Allow the canvas to dry completely.

4 Use the glow-in-the-dark fabric paint pen to write "In a galaxy far, far away" on the canvas and allow it to dry completely.

USE THE FORCE!

Type out your phrase in a word processing program (such as Word) and center the words. You can change the type size on each line to line up the words. Print this page out and use it as a guide for your art.

Jedi Party Favor Bags

WHAT YOU NEED:

- ✓ Brown lunch bags
- ✓ Construction paper: black, brown, and colors of your choice for lightsabers
- ✓ Scissors
- ✓ Glue stick
- ✓ Silver crayon

Host your next party like a real Jedi! Make your own Star Wars goodie bags to give out to all your guests.

1 Lay a paper bag out flat and crease the bottom flap downward.

2 Measure and cut a black construction paper strip 11½ cm x 1 cm.

3 Glue the black strip to the front of the bag, about 2½ cm or so above the bottom crease.

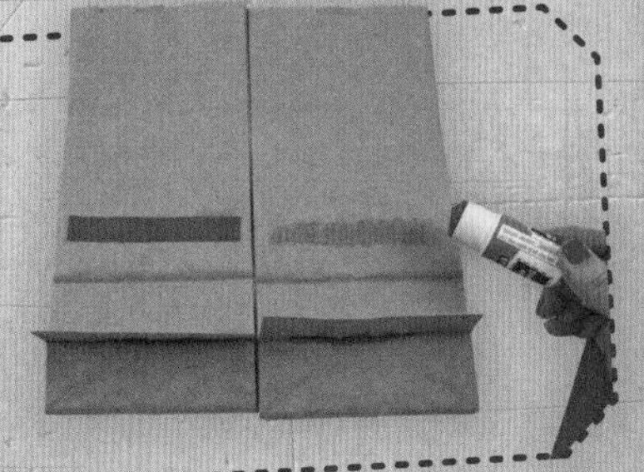

4 Measure and cut two brown construction paper strips, each 4 cm x 21 cm.

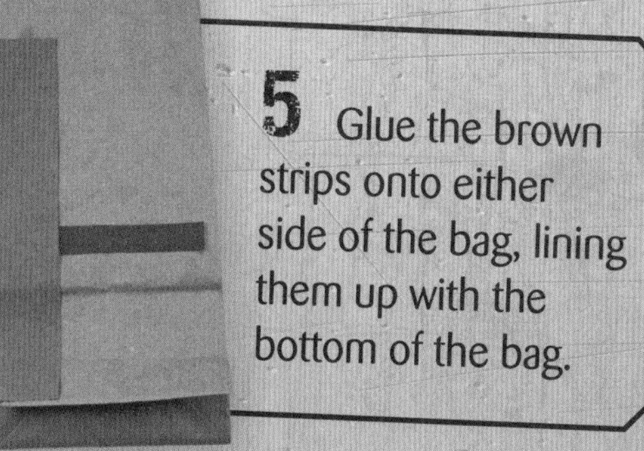

5 Glue the brown strips onto either side of the bag, lining them up with the bottom of the bag.

6 Now make the lightsaber. Measure and cut a piece of colored construction paper into a strip 15 cm x 1 cm.

7 Measure and cut black construction paper into a 1 cm x 2½ cm rectangle.

8 Glue the black rectangle to the end of the colored strip, and draw lines on the black using silver crayon.

9 Glue the lightsaber to the front of the bag on a diagonal.

WHAT YOU NEED:

- ✓ 2 paper plates
- ✓ Green paint
- ✓ Paintbrush
- ✓ Scissors
- ✓ 1 sheet white paper
- ✓ Pencil
- ✓ Black marker
- ✓ Glue stick
- ✓ Tape
- ✓ White and brown construction paper

Paper Plate Yoda

Yoda fan, you are? Decorate your party space with Yoda, you should.

1 Paint the back of two paper plates green, and let them dry.

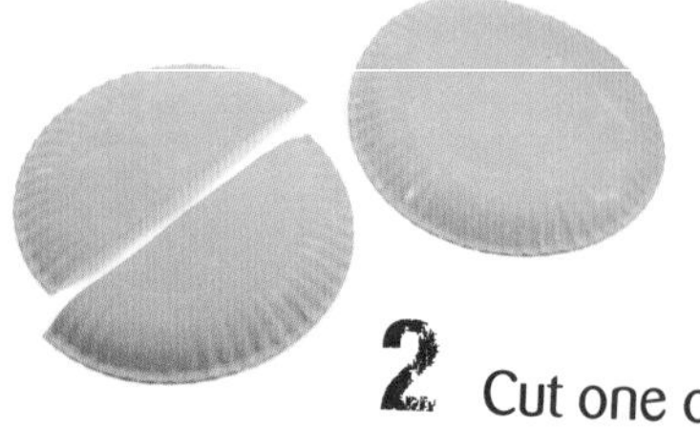

2 Cut one of the plates in half.

3 Cut one of those pieces in half. Use these pieces to cut curved ear shapes.

4 Cut the rim off of the remaining half, then cut the center into two pieces. From those two pieces, cut out ovals.

5 Fold the ovals in half and cut out the centers, leaving the ends connected. These are the eyelids.

6 Trace the inside of the green eyelids onto white paper. Draw a circle in the center of that pencil drawing, larger than the almond shape. Erase the lines outside the circles.

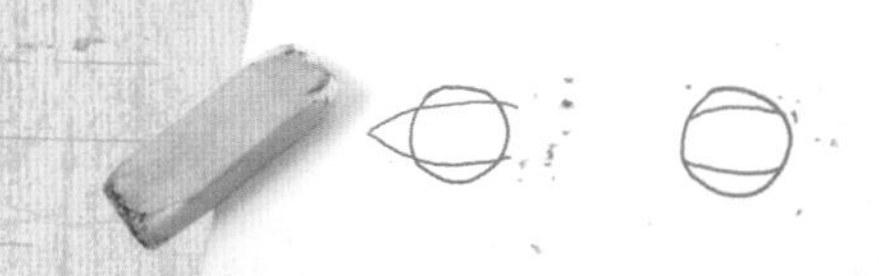

7 Color the circles black. Place the eyelid piece back over the circle and trace around it. Cut the ovals out, cutting inside the lines so that they are a little smaller than the eyelids.

8 Glue the eyeball to the eyelid on the inside.

9 Tape the ears to the back of the green plate.

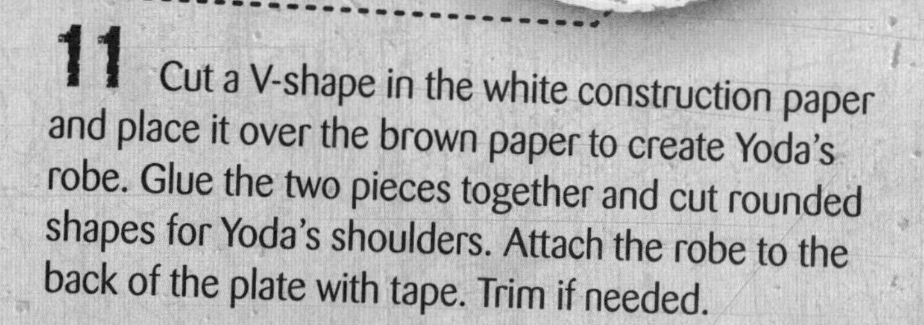

11 Cut a V-shape in the white construction paper and place it over the brown paper to create Yoda's robe. Glue the two pieces together and cut rounded shapes for Yoda's shoulders. Attach the robe to the back of the plate with tape. Trim if needed.

10 Glue the eyes in place on the green side of the plate. Use a marker to add a nose and mouth, and a pencil for details like wrinkles, eyebrows, and the inside of his ears.

FUN FACT:

Yoda was just over 60 cm tall but still one of the most powerful Jedi Masters. "Size matters not," Yoda reminded us.

Silhouette Party Banners

This banner is great for your next Star Wars party. In fact, making the banner could be a terrific party activity: Prepare the pieces in advance, and let your party guests create their own characters to add to the decorations.

WHAT YOU NEED:

- ✓ White printer paper
- ✓ Ruler
- ✓ Pencil
- ✓ Scissors
- ✓ Construction paper: white, green, black, yellow, brown
- ✓ Crayons: black, red, blue, silver, dark yellow
- ✓ Glue stick
- ✓ String

Make your Templates

1 For Yoda, you'll need two templates. Draw a small oval 9 cm x 6 cm on white printer paper. Cut this piece out. On another piece of paper, draw a 15 cm-long line. Draw a curved line from one end of line. Draw a curved line from one end of the line to the other, like a smile, to create a half-oval. Cut this piece out, too.

2 For R2-D2 and C-3P0, as well as the stormtrooper, draw a bigger oval, 11½ cm x 7½ cm, on white printer paper. Cut this out.

3 For Darth Vader and the stormtrooper, draw a circle 9 cm in diameter on white printer paper. You can use a bowl of the right size to make a neat circle.

4 For Darth Vader and the Jawa, draw a triangle 11½ cm high, with a 15 cm base, on white printer paper.

USE THE FORCE!

If you're going to be making several versions of each character, make your templates out of thin cardboard rather than white printer paper, so they're sturdier.

Yoda

1 Use the small oval and the half-oval templates to outline and then cut out these two shapes from green construction paper.

2 Glue the green oval over the green half-oval, as shown.

3 Draw two eyes with silver crayon.

C-3PO

1 Outline the bigger oval template on yellow construction paper and cut it out. Shape the oval into C-3PO's face by narrowing it at one end: Trim the lower left and right of the oval and snip off the bottom, as shown.

2 Draw two circles for eyes using dark yellow crayon.

3 Draw vertical lines in the eyes.

4 Draw a thick, straight, horizontal line for his mouth.

R2-D2

1 Use the bigger oval template to trace an oval on white construction paper. Cut the shape out, then cut the oval in half to make two chubby halves, as shown. This will make two R2-D2s.

2 Draw a circle for the radar eye with a silver crayon.

3 Draw a smaller circle below and to the left with red crayon.

4 Draw a few rectangles on the lower right with blue crayon.

Darth Vader

1 Use circle and triangle templates to cut both shapes from black paper.

2 Glue the circle on top of the triangle as shown.

3 Use a silver crayon to draw two eyes and the mask mouthguard.

Jawa

1 Use the triangle template to cut a triangle from brown paper.

2 Cut off the corners to round off all the ends.

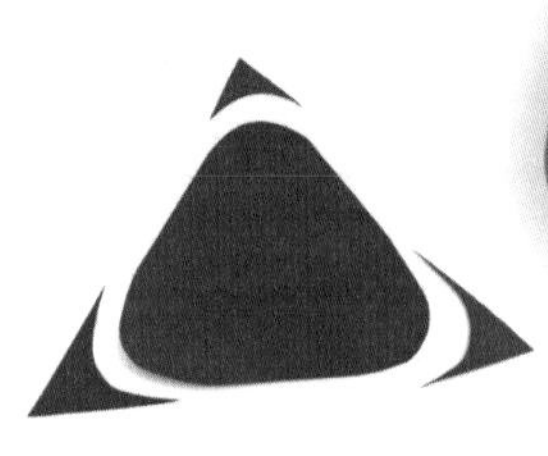

3 Draw eyes with a dark yellow crayon.

Stormtrooper

1 Use the circle template and the bigger oval template to cut these two shapes from white construction paper.

2 Trim the top of the circle to add a rounded point.

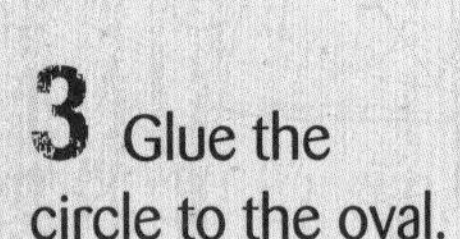

3 Glue the circle to the oval.

4 Draw eyes and mouth with black crayon.

Assemble

1 For each character, cut a strip from matching colored paper measuring 13 cm x 1 cm.

2 Glue one end to the back of the character, leaving 7½ cm free at the top.

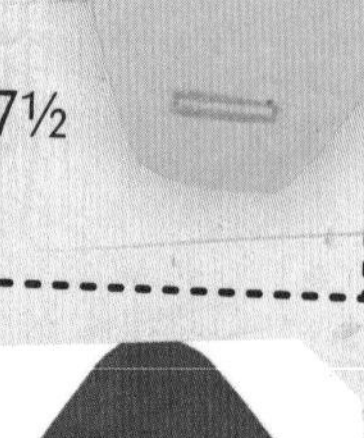

3 Lay out the string for your banner. Bend the strip around the string and secure to the back of each character with glue.

WHAT YOU NEED:

- ✓ Water bottle
- ✓ Felt: brown, tan, dark brown
- ✓ Scissors
- ✓ Hot glue gun
- ✓ Ruler

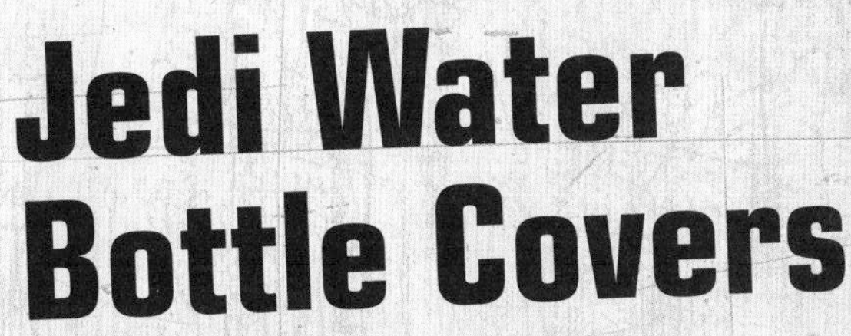

Jedi Water Bottle Covers

A Star Wars party wouldn't be complete without water bottles decked out in Jedi robes! The size of the cover will vary a little depending on the bottles you use, but they are easy to make and fun to drink from!

1 Measure and cut a piece of tan felt 10 cm high and wide enough to wrap around your bottle with 2½ cm of overlap.

2 Fold the tan felt rectangle in half, so the short ends meet, and cut off the top corner along the fold. This will create a triangle in the center of the felt for the neck.

3 Measure and cut a 13 cm high piece of brown felt roughly the same length as the tan felt.

4 Fold the brown felt, lining up the folded edge with the edge of the tan felt. Trim the brown felt as shown, so it is the same width as one side of the tan felt up to the neck.

5 Measure and cut a 1 cm x 13 cm strip of dark brown felt and glue to the tan felt below the v-neck.

6 Glue the tan felt around the water bottle.

7 Wrap the brown felt around the bottle as shown and glue in place.

Stormtrooper Placeholders

WHAT YOU NEED:

- ✓ Cardboard egg carton
- ✓ Scissors
- ✓ White paint
- ✓ Paintbrush
- ✓ Black marker
- ✓ Toothpicks
- ✓ White construction paper
- ✓ Glue stick or craft glue

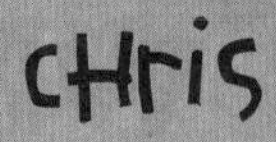

It's usually best to avoid Imperial stormtroopers, but if they're showing you where to sit at a party table, they're definitely welcome! Having the gang over for cake and ice cream? Set their places with these stormtroopers made from egg cartons!

1 Cut the egg cups from the egg carton and trim the edges so the cup sits flat, but leave the notches on the side.

2 Paint the outside of the egg cups white and allow to dry completely.

3 Use a black marker to draw on the mouthpiece of the mask and the eye area. Use a side of the egg cup that has a cutaway notch, which is similar to the stormtrooper helmet shape.

4 Cut strips of white construction paper. Wrap each strip around the top of a toothpick and secure it with glue. Write names on these flags and insert into the top of the stormtrooper's helmet.

STUFF FOR YOUR ROOM

Star Wars Window Clings

WHAT YOU NEED:

- ✓ *Star Wars* logo print-out
- ✓ Cutting board or other hard mobile surface
- ✓ Parchment paper or wax paper
- ✓ Tape
- ✓ Gold and black puffy paint

Window clings are fun and easy to make and you need only a few materials. And once you learn this technique, you can make any Star Wars *art in the universe to decorate your windows. However, as Yoda says, "Patience you must have, my young Padawan." The puffy paint needs to dry overnight before you can use your new window cling!*

USE THE FORCE!

Puffy paint is available from many arts and crafts stores and online. It's also sometimes known as 3-D fabric paint. Be careful when you're making your window cling—it can stain your clothes.

1 Find a version of the *Star Wars* logo that you like, and use this as a stencil. You can even use the one on the front cover of this book! Place the logo on your cutting board, and tape a sheet of parchment paper or wax paper on top.

2 Trace the letters using gold puffy paint. Be sure there are no gaps.

3 Fill in the letters completely, making sure there are no holes or gaps.

4 Trace the outline of the letters with black puffy paint.

5 Connect all the letters together with the black puffy paint, as shown, to ensure that the window cling is one solid piece.

6 Allow the paint to dry overnight. If you've applied the paint very thickly, it may take a little longer to dry. Once it's completely dry, you can carefully peel your window cling from the parchment paper.

7 Press the window cling onto a clean, dry window or mirror.

WHAT YOU NEED:

- ✓ Craft sticks
- ✓ Craft paint: white, black, silver
- ✓ Glitter craft paint in colors of your choice
- ✓ Toothpick

Lightsaber Bookmarks

Use the Force—keep your place in your favorite books with glittery lightsabers in different colors. These are great for home or school, or as gifts for all your friends.

1 Paint the craft sticks white on both sides, and let them dry completely.

2 Painting one side at a time, cover all but the end with your choice of glitter craft paint. Let dry and repeat on the other side. Paint a second coat if needed. Let dry.

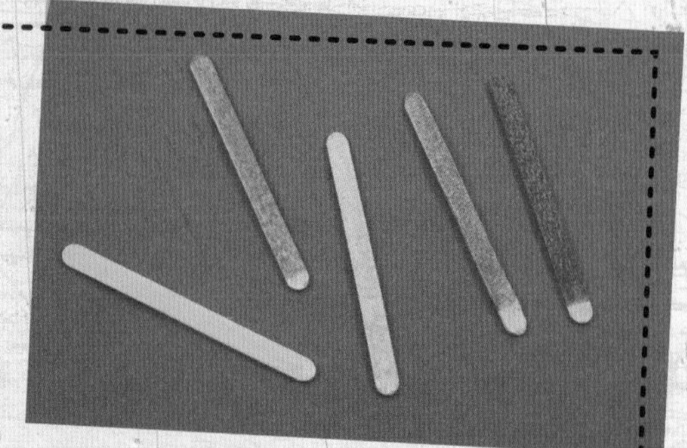

3 Paint the end of the stick black on both sides.

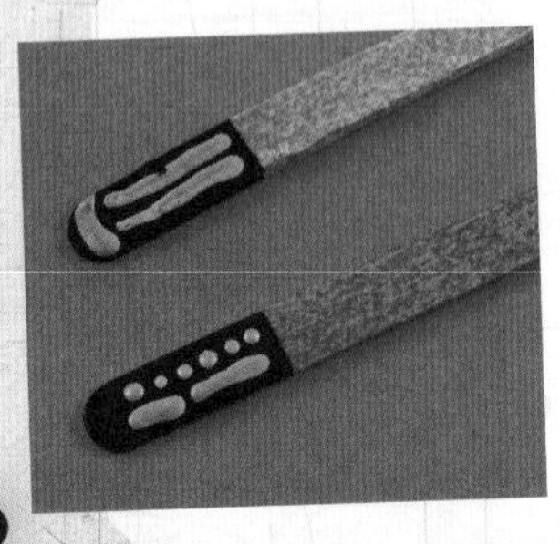

4 Use a toothpick dipped in silver paint to add dots and/or lines to the black handles on both sides.

FUN FACT:

To use a lightsaber, you need a very high level of skill and strength. The blade consisted of pure energy, which is very hot and can be controlled only by those who are expert in the ways of the Force.

Universe Picture Frame

Make a picture frame that's out of this world by learning how to paint a galaxy! This is a great method, one that we can use to make a Galaxy Hat (page 16) and add special starry accents to other projects.

WHAT YOU NEED:

- ✓ Wooden picture frame
- ✓ Paint: black, light blue, blue, purple, light purple, white
- ✓ Paintbrush
- ✓ Scruffy paintbrush
- ✓ Old toothbrush
- ✓ Toothpick
- ✓ Paper towel or an old cloth
- ✓ Clear acrylic spray sealer, matte finish

1 Paint the frame black. Let this paint dry.

2 Dip an old paintbrush into light blue paint. Press the paintbrush into the paper towel and move in a circular motion to remove most of the excess paint. Apply the "dry" brush to the frame in different areas to create splotches.

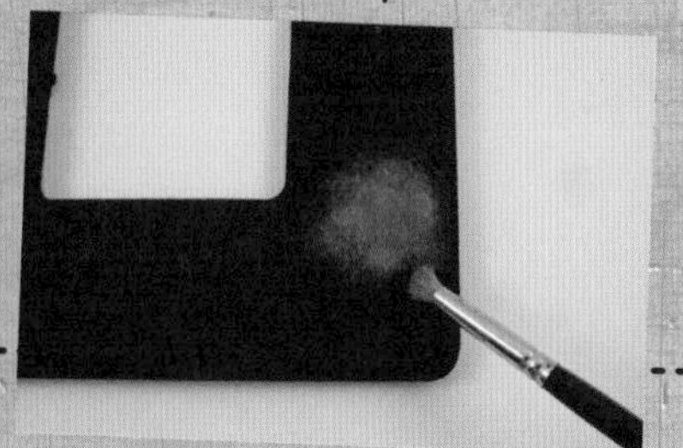

3 Repeat step 2 with blue, purple, and light purple paint to achieve the galaxy look.

4 Dip the bristles of the toothbrush into water and dab off the excess onto a paper towel. Dip the toothbrush bristles into white paint and dab off excess onto a paper towel. Drag your thumb or finger across the bristles, releasing speckles of paint. Apply the stars to the frame using this toothbrush method.

5 Dip a toothpick into white paint and dot paint onto the frame in random areas to add some bright stars.

6 When the frame has dried completely, apply a coat of acrylic sealer and let dry.

USE THE FORCE!

Practice your star-making on a piece of scrap paper first, to get the technique down before you add stars to your picture frame.

WHAT YOU NEED:

- ✓ Flat-topped Styrofoam cone
- ✓ Red felt
- ✓ Scissors
- ✓ Hot glue gun or felt glue
- ✓ Wooden skewer
- ✓ Craft knife
- ✓ Brown marker
- ✓ Silver and black paint

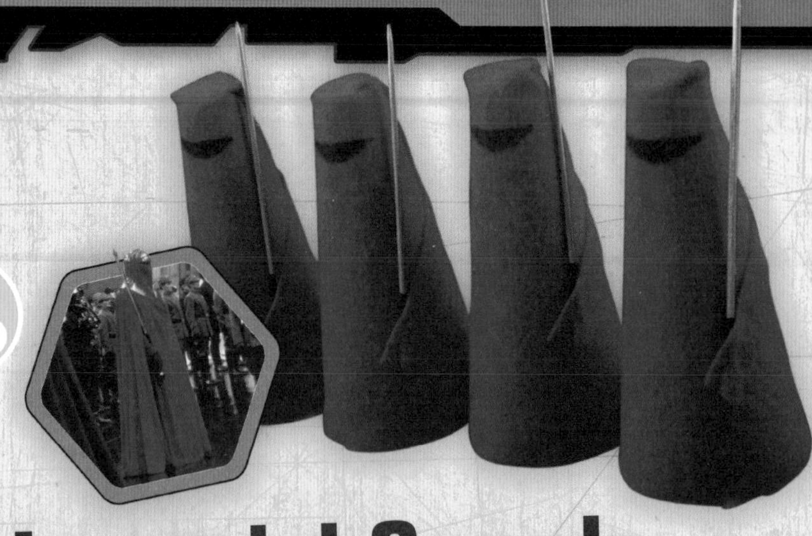

Imperial Guards

If they are elite enough to protect the Emperor, they are definitely worthy of a high shelf in your room! Make a set of your very own Imperial Guards to keep watch over you and your stuff at all times.

1 Cover the Styrofoam cone with red felt, trimming off the excess and gluing down the edges with felt glue or a hot glue gun.

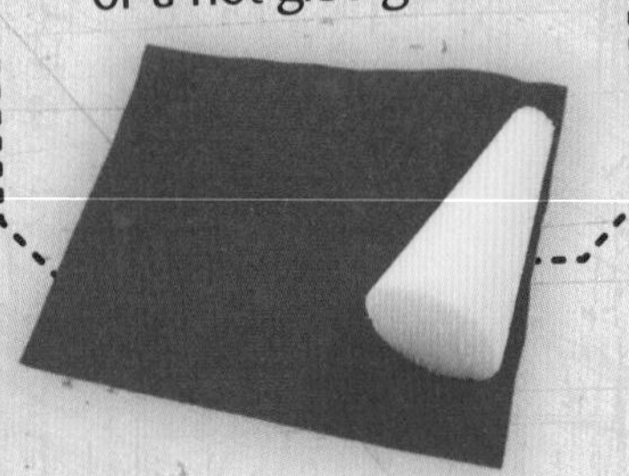

2 To make the "force pike," use a craft knife to trim a few centimetres from the wooden skewer, so it's a good size for your Imperial Guard.

3 Trim the pointed end, making it blunt (so you don't stick yourself) but not flat.

4 Paint the skewer silver.

5 Paint about 5 cm of the flat end of the skewer black.

6 Make a face mask for your guard by drawing half of an oval onto the red felt.

7 Glue the pike to the side of the Guard.

8 From some red felt, cut a strip approximately 10 cm x 2 cm and glue one end over the black handle of the pike and glue the rest of the strip around the back of the Guard's body.

Jawa Rocks

If you ever get the chance to visit the planet Tatooine, chances are you will run into clans of roving Jawas. If you have a droid with you, be sure to keep it close by. Jawas are famous for scavenging old equipment and selling it to whoever will buy!

WHAT YOU NEED:

- ✓ Smooth rocks, washed and dried
- ✓ Sandpaper (if needed)
- ✓ Acrylic craft paint: black, brown, dark yellow
- ✓ Paintbrush
- ✓ Round sponge applicator
- ✓ Fine point black permanent marker

NOTE: You can find smooth rocks out in your yard or at the park. You can also purchase rocks from the craft store but these rocks will probably have been polished. Use a piece of sandpaper to knock off the shine so that the paint can stick more easily.

1 Paint the rocks with two coats of brown paint, allowing them to dry between coats.

2 Use a round sponge applicator to apply black paint to one end of the rock for the Jawa's face.

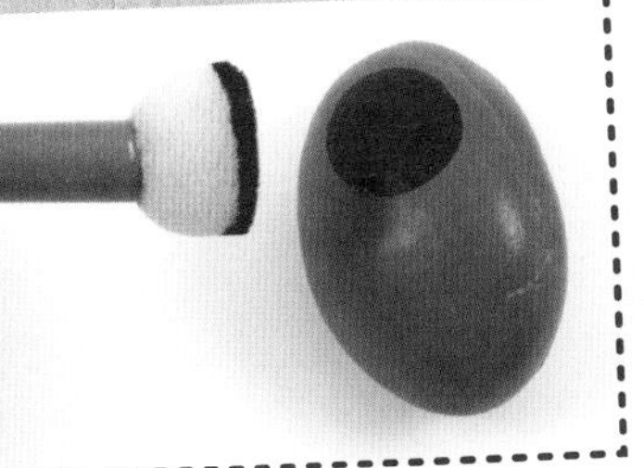

3 Using the handle end of your paintbrush dipped in dark yellow paint, add two eyes to the black paint.

4 Use a marker to draw squares for the ammo pouches on the Jawa's bandolier. Add a triangle for the pouch flap. Draw several in a row and connect them together with simple lines.

USE THE FORCE!

If you would like to keep your Jawas outside, use an outdoor craft paint, such as Patio Paint.

WHAT YOU NEED:

- ✓ Tin can
- ✓ Felt: gray, white, blue, red, black
- ✓ Felt glue
- ✓ Scissors

R2-D2 Pencil Holder

With his beeps and blips and special bravery, R2-D2 is everyone's favorite droid. Now you can have him on your desk all the time with your very own pencil holder.

1 Cover the can with one layer of white felt, tucking the excess felt inside the can to cover any sharp edges.

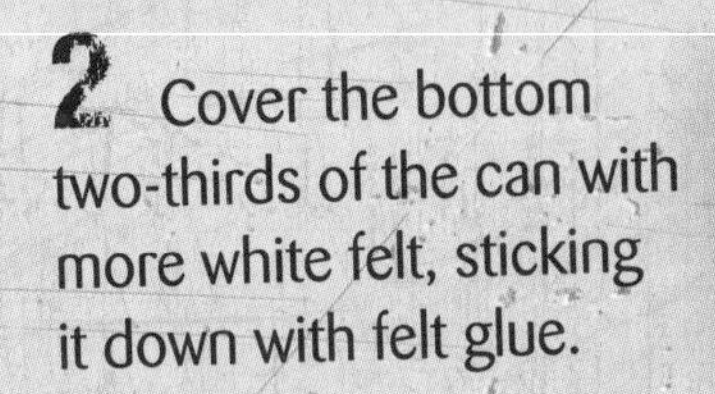

2 Cover the bottom two-thirds of the can with more white felt, sticking it down with felt glue.

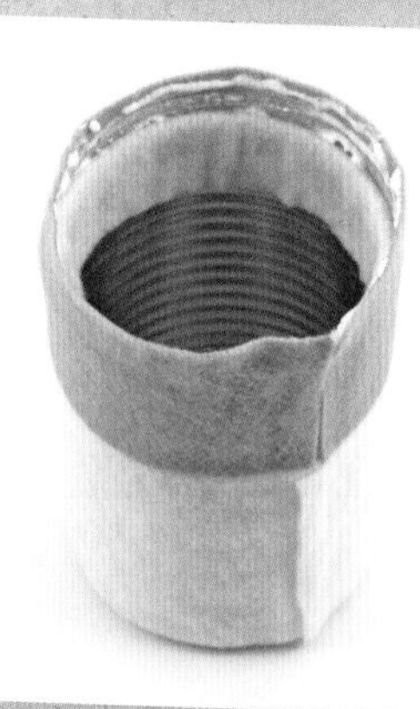

3 Cover the top third of the can with gray felt. Glue any excess felt inside the can.

4 Cut a long, thin strip of blue felt and wrap it around the can where the gray and white felt meet.

5 Cut small rectangles from blue felt to create the blue sections of the droid.

6 Glue rectangles around the gray top section, gluing one larger rectangle in the center for R2-D2's camera lens. Cut a black circle for the lens, and glue it in place.

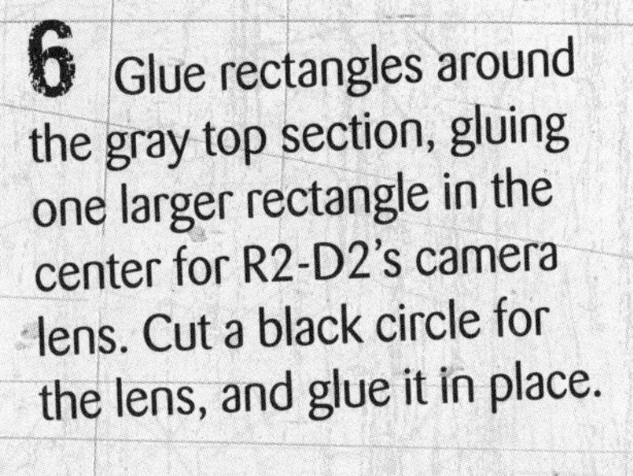

7 Glue a small red circle below the camera, and glue three long blue strips in the white section.

8 Glue three gray rectangles below the blue strips.

9 Attach clothespins around the rim of the can to secure the felt in place while the glue dries, about an hour or so.

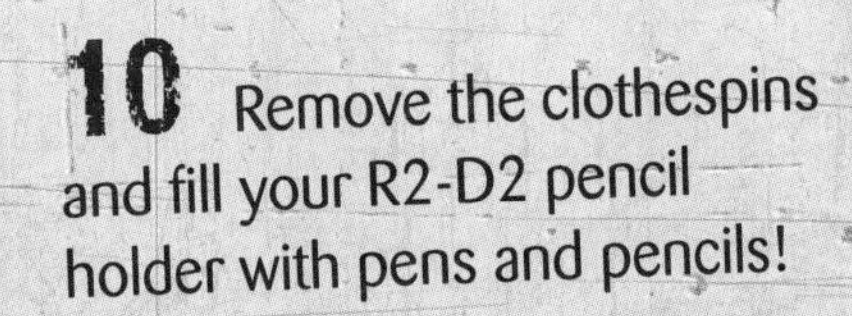

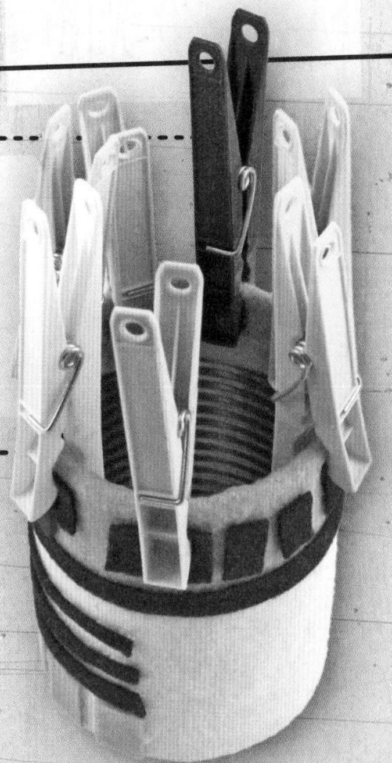

10 Remove the clothespins and fill your R2-D2 pencil holder with pens and pencils!

FUN FACT:

Technically, R2-D2 is an astromech droid, equipped with a powerful computer as well as all kind of gadgets, tools, and sensors. He is small but he is very brave, never hesitating in the face of danger. His three legs allow him to cross different types of terrain—he can either walk on two of his legs or roll on all three.

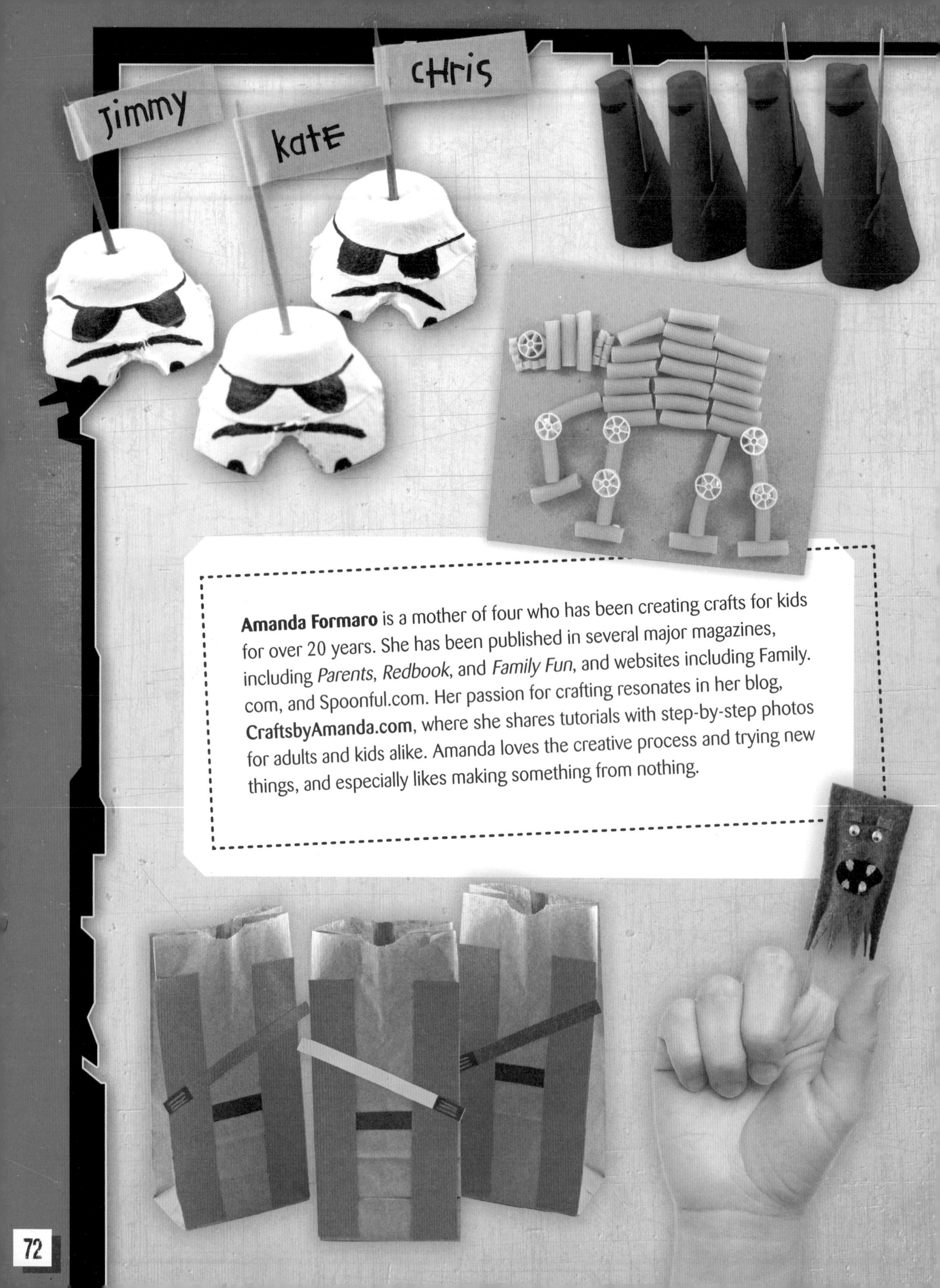

Amanda Formaro is a mother of four who has been creating crafts for kids for over 20 years. She has been published in several major magazines, including *Parents*, *Redbook*, and *Family Fun*, and websites including Family.com, and Spoonful.com. Her passion for crafting resonates in her blog, **CraftsbyAmanda.com**, where she shares tutorials with step-by-step photos for adults and kids alike. Amanda loves the creative process and trying new things, and especially likes making something from nothing.